credits

DESIGNER:
Martin Storey

PHOTOGRAPHY
Quail Studio

ART DIRECTION & STYLING
Georgina Brant

DESIGN LAYOUT
Quail Studio

MODEL
Daysey and Louis

HAIR & MAKEUP
Michelle - Court-on-Camera Creatives

KNITTERS
Cath·Jazz·Cher·Lucy·Nicola·
Vivienne·Jackie·Janet·Jane
Sandra·Emma·Judith
Martinette·Jacqui
Ann·Tracey

First published in Great Britain in 2022 by
Quail Publishing Limited
Unit 15, Green Farm, Fritwell, Bicester, Oxfordshire,
OX27 7QU
E-mail: info@quailstudio.co.uk

ISBN: 978-1-8384102-2-3

EASY
STYLE

designed by
martin storey

quail studio

INTRO

Welcome to my Easy Style collection. Easy Style includes 12 designs aimed at those beginner knitters looking to advance to the next level. Basic stocking stitch combined with simple to knit lace, cable and textured stitches feature, to create a fun, cosy and easy to wear collection of garments and cosy accessories.

All twelve designs are knitted in Rowan's popular and super soft, Big Wool. For this collection I've introduced a new, winter pastel palette including Melon, Nougat pink, Floss and Limeade green.

Martin
x

boogie hat pattern page 34

boogie cowl pattern page 36

buzz pattern page 38

comfy pattern page 40

dash pattern page 44

frothy pattern page 46

mellow pattern page 50

swish pattern page 52

whisper pattern page 54

whoosh pattern page 58

zap pattern page 60

zoom pattern page 62

BOOGIE HAT

PAGE 34

BOOGIE COWL

PAGE 36

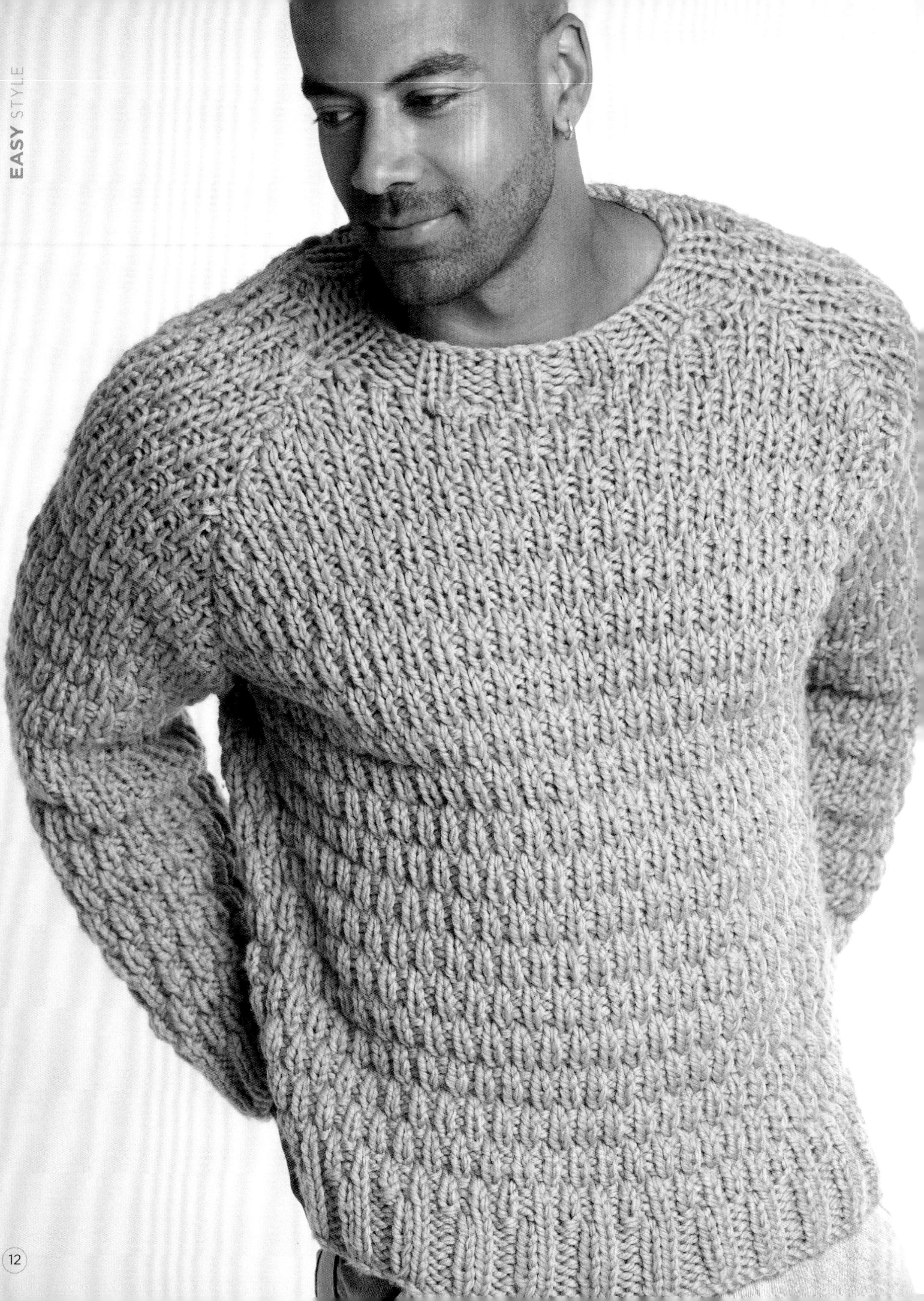

BUZZ

PAGE 38

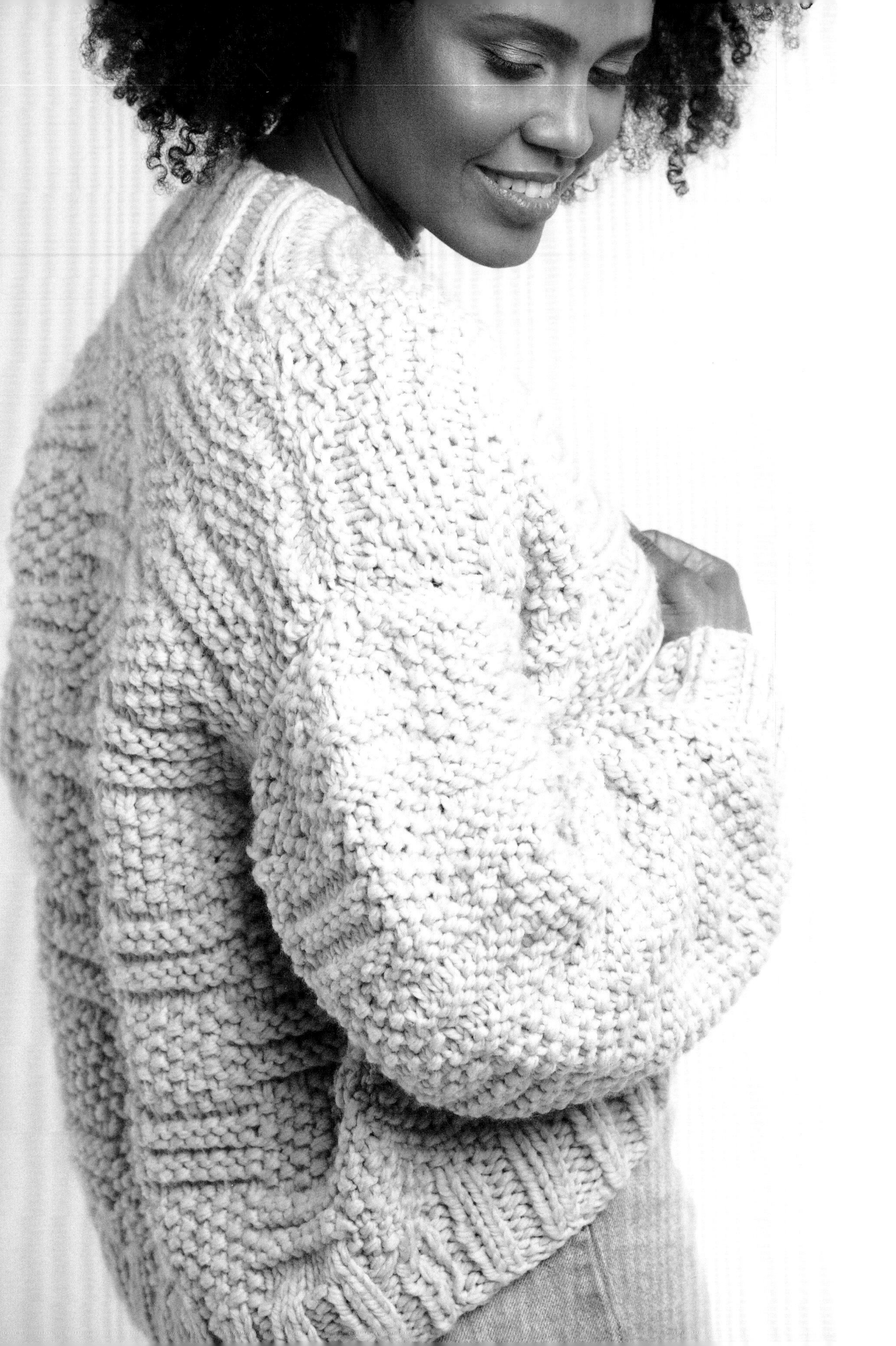

COMFY

PAGE 40

DASH

PAGE 44

FROTHY

PAGE 46

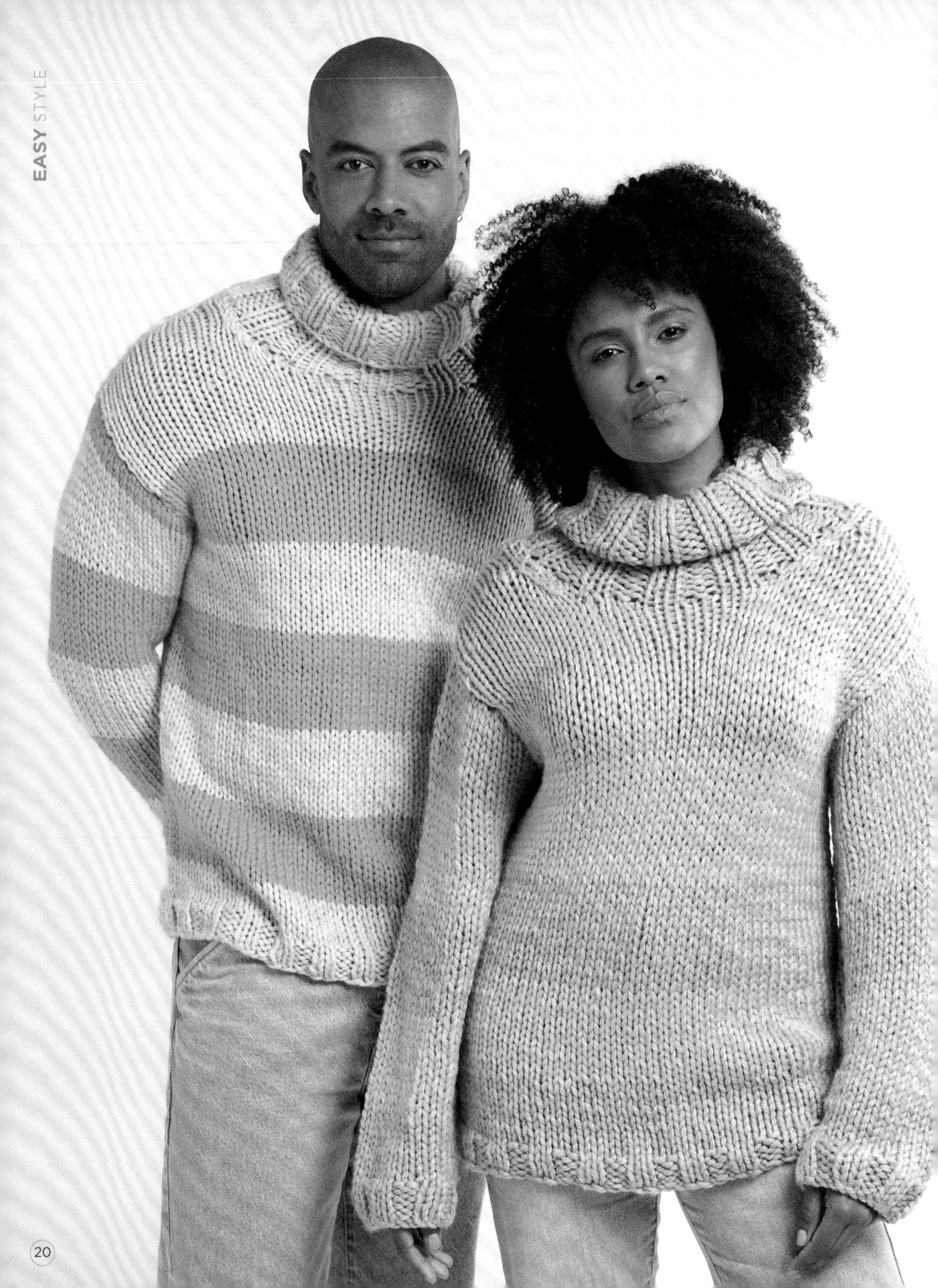

MELLOW

PAGE 50

SWISH

PAGE 52

WHISPER

PAGE 54

WHOOSH

PAGE 58

ZAP

PAGE 60

ZOOM

PAGE 62

BOOGIE HAT

SIZE
To fit an average adult head
Circumference 51 cm (20 in)

YARN
Big Wool
1 x 100gm
(photographed in Melon 094, Floss 097, Limeade 096
& Nougat 095)

NEEDLES
1 pair 10mm (no 000) (US 15) needles

TENSION
10 sts and 14 rows to 10 cm measured over patt st
using 10mm (US 15) needles.

HAT
Using 10mm (US 15) needles, cast on 50 sts.
Next row (RS): * K2, P2, rep from * to last 2 sts, K2.
Next row (WS): * P2, K2, rep from * to last 2 sts, P2.
These 2 rows form rib.
Work in rib until work meas 7 cm from beg, ending on
a WS row and inc 1 st at end of last row. 51 sts.
Row 1 (RS): Knit.
Row 2 (WS): Purl.
Row 3: As Row 1.
Row 4: As Row 2.
Row 5: K1, *P1, K1, rep from * to end.
Row 6: P1, *K1, P1, rep from * to end.
These 6 rows form patt.
Starting with a K row, cont in st st until work meas
14 cm from cast on, ending on a WS row and dec
1 st at end of last row. 50 sts.
Shape crown
Working in st st throughout:
Next row (RS): * K8, K2tog, rep from * to end. 45 sts.
Next row and every foll alt row (WS): Purl.
Next row: *K7, K2tog, rep from * to end. 40 sts.
Next row: *K6, K2tog, rep from * to end. 35 sts.
Next row: *K5, K2tog, rep from * to end. 30 sts.
Next row: *K4, K2tog, rep from * to end. 25 sts.
Next row: *K3, K2tog, rep from * to end. 20 sts.
Next row: *K2, K2tog, rep from * to end. 15 sts.
Next row: *K1, K2tog, rep from * to end. 10 sts.
Next row: (K2tog) 5 times. 5 sts.
Break yarn leaving a long tail for joining back seam.
Thread through rem 5 sts and pull up tight and fasten
off securely.

MAKING UP
Press as described on the information page.
Join back seam using mattress stitch.

BOOGIE COWL

SIZE
Approx circumference 80 cm (31½ in) x 56 cm (22 in) deep.

YARN
Big Wool
4x 100gm
(photographed in Melon 094, Floss 097, Limeade 096
& Nougat 095)

NEEDLES
1 pair 10mm (no 000) (US 15) needles

TENSION
10 sts and 14 rows to 10 cm measured over patt st
using 10mm (US 15) needles.

COWL
Using 10mm (US 15) needle, cast on 82 sts.
Next row (RS): * K2, P2, rep from * to last 2 sts, K2.
Next row (WS): * P2, K2, rep from * to last 2 sts, P2.
These 2 rows form rib.
Work in rib for a further 3 rows, ending on a RS row
and with WS facing for next row.
Next row (WS): Keeping rib correct throughout,
dec 1 st at end of row. 81 sts.
Row 1 (RS): Knit.
Row 2 (WS): Purl.
Row 3: As Row 1.
Row 4: As Row 2.
Row 5: K1, * P1, K1, rep from * to end.
Row 6: P1, * K1, P1, rep from * to end.
These 6 rows form patt.
Rep rows 1-6 a further 10 times, then rows 1 – 4 once
more, inc 1 st at end of last row. 82 sts.
Next row (RS): * K2, P2, rep from * to last 2 sts, K2.
Next row (WS): * P2, K2, rep from * to last 2 sts, P2.
These 2 rows form rib.
Work in rib for a further 3 rows, ending on a RS row
and with WS facing for next row.
Cast off loosely in rib.

MAKING UP
Press as described on the information page.
Join back seam using mattress stitch.

BUZZ

○ ● ●

SIZE
To fit bust

71-76	81-86	91-97	102-107	112-117	122-127	132-137	142-147	152-157	cm
28-30	32-34	36-38	40-42	44-46	48-50	52-54	56-58	60-62	in

Actual bust measurement of garment

85	97	105	116	127	135	146	158	169	cm
33¾	38¼	41¼	45¾	50¼	53¼	57¾	62¼	66¾	in

YARN
Big Wool

9	9	10	10	11	11	12	12	13	x 100gm

(photographed in Concrete 061)

NEEDLES
1 pair 10mm (no 000) (US 15) needles

TENSION
10.5 sts and 13.5 rows to 10 cm measured over patt st using 10mm (US 15) needles.

EXTRAS
Stitch holders

BACK
Using 10mm (US 15) needles, cast on 46 [54: 58: 62: 70: 74: 78: 86: 90] sts.
Next row (RS): * K2, P2, rep from * to last 2 sts, K2.
Next row (WS): * P2, K2, rep from * to last 2 sts, P2.
These 2 rows form rib.
Work in rib for a further 5 rows, ending on a RS row and with WS facing for next row.
Next row (WS): Keeping rib throughout, inc [dec: dec: inc: dec: dec: inc: dec: inc] 1 st at end of row. 47 [53: 57: 63: 69: 73: 79: 85: 91] sts.
Row 1 (RS): P1, * K1, P1, rep from * to end.
Row 2: K1, * P1, K1, rep from * to end.
Row 3: As row 1.
Row 4: Purl.
Row 5: K1, * P1, K1, rep from * to end.
Row 6: P1, * K1, P1, rep from * to end.
Row 7: As row 5.
Row 8: Purl.
These 8 rows form broken rib patt.
Work in patt as set until work measures 40 [41: 41.5: 42: 42.5: 43: 43: 44: 44] cm from cast on, ending on a WS row and with RS facing for next row.
Shape raglan armholes
Starting with a RS row and keeping patt correct throughout, cast off 3 sts at beg of next 2 rows.
41 [47: 51: 57: 63: 67: 73: 79: 85] sts.
Starting with a RS row and keeping patt correct throughout, dec 1 st at each end of every alt row 12 [9: 9: 9: 8: 8: 7: 7: 3] times, then on every row 2 [8: 10: 12: 16: 18: 22: 25: 32] times, ending on a WS row and with RS facing for next row. 13 [13: 13: 15: 15: 15: 15: 15: 15] sts.
Break yarn and slip sts on a holder for back neck.

FRONT
Work as for back until 8 [8: 8: 8: 8: 10: 10: 10: 12] rows less have been worked to end of raglan armhole shaping, ending on a WS row and with RS facing for next row. 23 [29: 29: 31: 31: 35: 35: 35: 39] sts.
Shape neck
Sizes 71-76, 81-86, 91-97, 102-107, 112-117 cm ONLY
Next row (RS): Dec 1 st at armhole edge, patt 4 [7: 7: 7: 7] sts, K2tog and turn, leaving rem sts on a stitch holder. 6 [9: 9: 9: 9] sts.
* **Next row (WS):** Cast off 1 [2: 2: 2: 2] sts at neck edge, and dec 1 st at armhole edge. 4 [6: 6: 6: 6] sts.
Next row: Dec 1 st at each end. 2 [4: 4: 4: 4] sts.
Next row: Cast off 0 [1: 1: 1: 1] st at neck edge, and dec 0 [1: 1: 1: 1] st at armhole edge. 2 sts.
Next row: K2tog and fasten off. **
With RS facing, slip next 7 [7: 7: 9: 9] sts onto a stitch holder for centre front neck, rejoin yarn, K2tog, patt to last 2 sts, dec 1 st at armhole edge. 6 [9: 9: 9: 9] sts.
Rep from * to **, reversing shapings to match first side.
Sizes 122-127, 132-137, 142-147 cm ONLY
Next row (RS): Dec 1 st at armhole edge, patt 9 sts, K2tog and turn, leaving rem sts on a stitch holder. 11 sts.
* **Next row (WS):** dec 1 st at each end. 9 sts.
Rep last row 3 times more. 3 sts.
Next row: dec 1 st at armhole edge. 2 sts.
Next row: K2tog and fasten off. **
With RS facing, slip next 9 sts onto a stitch holder for centre front neck, rejoin yarn, K2tog, patt to last 2 sts, dec 1 st at armhole edge. 11 sts.
Rep from * to **, reversing shapings to match first side.
Size 152-157 cm ONLY
Next row (RS): Dec 1 st at armhole edge, patt 11 sts, K2tog and turn, leaving rem sts on a stitch holder. 13 sts.

* **Next row (WS):** dec 1 st at each end. 11 sts.
Rep last row 3 times more. 5 sts.
Next row: dec 1 st at armhole edge. 4 sts.
Rep last row twice more. 2 sts.
Next row: K2tog and fasten off. **
With RS facing, slip next 9 sts onto a stitch holder for
centre front neck, rejoin yarn, K2tog, patt to last 2 sts,
dec 1 st at armhole edge. 13 sts.
Rep from * to **, reversing shapings to match first side.

SLEEVES

Using 10mm (US 15) needles, cast on 30 [30: 30: 30:
30: 30: 30: 34: 34] sts.
Next row (RS): * K2, P2, rep from * to last 2 sts, K2.
Next row (WS): * P2, K2, rep from * to last 2 sts, P2.
These 2 rows form rib.
Work in rib for a further 5 rows, ending on a RS row
and with WS facing for next row.
Next row (WS): Keeping rib correct throughout,
dec [dec: dec: inc: inc: inc: inc: dec: dec] 1 st at end
of row. 29 [29: 29: 31: 31: 31: 31: 33: 33] sts.
Starting with a RS row, work in broken rib patt as set
for back, inc 1 st at each end of every 6th [5th: 4th: 4th:
3rd: 2nd: 2nd: next: next] RS row 4 [5: 5: 4: 6: 7:
13: 2: 4] times, then on every - [-: 5th: 5th: 4th: 3rd: -: 2nd:
2nd] RS row - [-: 1: 2: 2: 4: -: 12: 11] times. 37 [39: 41: 43:
47: 53: 57: 61: 63] sts.
Keeping patt correct throughout, cont working straight
until work meas 46 [47: 47: 48: 48: 48: 48: 48: 48] cm
from cast on, ending on a WS row and with RS facing
for next row.

Shape raglan

Starting with a RS row and keeping patt correct
throughout, cast off 3 sts at beg of next 2 rows.
31 [33: 35: 37: 41: 47: 51: 55: 57] sts.
Starting with a RS row and keeping patt correct
throughout, dec 1 st at each end of every 3rd [3rd: 3rd: 3rd:
2nd: 2nd: 2nd: 2nd: 2nd] row 2 [2: 2: 2: 15: 14: 14: 13: 13] times,
then on every 2nd [2nd: 2nd: 2nd: -: next: next: next: next]
row 8 [9: 10: 11: -: 4: 6: 9: 10] times, ending on a WS row
and with RS facing for next row. 11 sts.

Right sleeve only

Next row (RS): Cast off 3 sts at beg and dec 1 st at end
of row. 7 sts
Next row (WS): dec 1 st at beg of row. 6 sts.
Next row: Cast off 3 sts at beg and dec 1 st at end
of row. 2 sts
Cast off rem 2 sts.

Left sleeve only

Next row (RS): dec 1 st, patt to end. 10 sts
Next row (WS): cast off 3 sts, and dec 1 st at end
of row. 6 sts.
Next row: dec 1 st, patt to end. 5 sts.
Next row: cast off 3 sts, patt to end. 2 sts.
Cast off rem 2 sts.

MAKING UP

Press as described on the information page.
Join both front and right back raglan seams using back
stitch, or mattress stitch if preferred.

Neckband

With RS facing and using 10mm (US 15) needle, starting
at left shoulder, pick up and knit 2 sts from top of
sleeve cap, 4 sts down left sleeve, 5 [5: 5: 5: 5: 7: 7:
7: 9] sts down left front neck, knit 7 [7: 7: 9: 9: 9: 9:
9: 9] sts from front neck sts on holder, pick up and knit
5 [5: 5: 5: 5: 7: 7: 7: 9] sts up right front neck, 4 sts up
right sleeve, 2 sts from top of sleeve cap, and knit
13 [13: 13: 15: 15: 15: 15: 15: 15] sts from back neck sts
on holder. 42 [42: 42: 46: 46: 50: 50: 50: 54] sts.
Next row (WS): *P2, K2, rep from * to last 2 sts, P2.
Next row (RS): *K2, P2, rep from * to last 2 sts, K2.
These 2 rows form rib.
Work in rib for a further 2 rows, ending on a RS row
and with WS facing for next row.
Cast off in rib.
Sew up left back and neck seams.

Join sleeves and side seams using back stitch,
or mattress stitch if preferred.

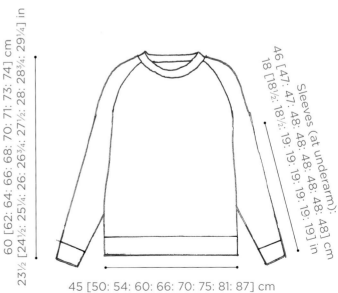

60 [62: 64: 66: 68: 70: 71: 73: 74] cm
23½ [24½: 25¼: 26: 26¾: 27½: 28: 28¾: 29¼] in

Sleeves (at underarm):
46 [47: 47: 48: 48: 48: 48: 48: 48] cm
18 [18½: 18½: 19: 19: 19: 19: 19: 19] in

45 [50: 54: 60: 66: 70: 75: 81: 87] cm
17¾ [19¾: 21¼: 23½: 26: 27½: 29½: 32: 34¼] in

COMFY

SIZE
To fit bust

71-76	81-86	91-97	102-107	112-117	122-127	132-137	142-147	152-157	cm
28-30	32-34	36-38	40-42	44-46	48-50	52-54	56-58	60-62	in

Actual bust measurement of garment

99	116	120	128	145	154	162	175	183	cm
39¾	46½	48	51½	58	61¼	64¾	68	74½	in

YARN
Big Wool

9	10	10	11	12	12	13	14	14	x 100gm

(photographed in Floss 097)

NEEDLES
1 pair 10mm (no 000) (US 15) needles
10mm (no 000) (US 15) circular needle at least 120 cm long.

TENSION
9.5 sts and 17 rows to 10 cm measured over patt st
using 10mm (US 15) needles.

EXTRAS
Stitch markers
Stitch holders

Texture Pattern
Row 1 (RS): *(K1, P1) twice, K7, P1, K1, P1, rep from * to last st, K1.
Row 2 (WS): K1, *P1, K1, P9, K1, P1, K1, rep from * to end.
Row 3: *K1, P1, K1, P9, K1, P1, rep from * to last st, K1.
Row 4: K1, *P1, K1, P1, K7, (P1, K1) twice, rep from * to end.
Row 5: As row 1.
Row 6: As row 2.
Row 7: As row 3.
Row 8: As row 4.
Row 9: As row 1.
Row 10: As row 2.
Row 11: *K4, (P1, K1) 4 times, K2, rep from * to last st, K1.
Row 12: P1, *P4, (K1, P1) 3 times, P4, rep from * to end.
Row 13: *P5, (K1, P1) twice, K1, P4, rep from * to last st, P1
Row 14: K1 *K3, (P1, K1) 3 times, P1, K4, rep from * to end.
Row 15: As row 11.
Row 16: As row 12.
Row 17: As row 13.
Row 18: As row 14.
Row 19: As row 11.
Row 20: As row 12.
These rows form the texture pattern
Rep rows 1-20 throughout.

BACK
Using 10mm (US 15) needles, cast on 50 [58: 58: 62: 70: 74: 78: 82: 90] sts.

Next row (RS): * K2, P2, rep from * to last 2 sts, K2.
Next row (WS): * P2, K2, rep from * to last 2 sts, P2.
These 2 rows form rib.
Work in rib for a further 7 rows, ending on a RS row and with WS facing for next row.
Next row (WS): Keeping rib patt correct throughout, dec [dec: inc: inc: inc: inc: inc: inc: dec] 1 [1: 1: 1: 1: 1: 1: 3: 1] st(s) evenly across the row. 49 [57: 59: 63: 71: 75: 79: 85: 89] sts.
With RS facing, place a stitch marker 3 [-: 1: 3: -: 2: 4: -: 2] st(s) in from both edges. These markers will set the edge sts worked in moss st throughout.
Row 1 (RS): P 1 [-: 1: 1: -: 0: 0: -: 0], (K1, P1) 1 [-: 0: 1: -: 1: 2: -: 1] times, work texture patt as set until 3 [-: 1: 3: -: 2: 4: -: 2] st(s) remain, (P1, K1) 1 [-: 0: 1: -: 1: 2: -: 1] times, P 1 [-: 1: 1: -: 0: 0: -: 0].
Last row sets moss stitch edging with texture patt, work as set until work meas
29 [30.5: 30.5: 32: 32: 32: 32: 33: 33] cm from cast on, ending on a WS row and with RS facing for next row.
Armhole shaping
Starting with RS facing and keeping patt correct throughout, cast off 2 [3: 3: 4: 4: 5: 5: 6: 7] sts at beg of next 2 rows, then 1 [1: 1: 1: 2: 2: 2: 3: 3] sts at beg of next 2 rows, then 1 [1: 1: 1: 1: 2: 2: 2] sts at beg of next 2 rows, then dec 1 st at beg of next 0 [4: 4: 4: 4: 4: 4: 4: 4] rows. 41 [43: 45: 47: 53: 55: 57: 59: 61] sts.
Keeping patt correct throughout, cont working straight until work meas 22 [24: 24: 26: 26: 30: 30: 32: 32] cm from beg of armhole shaping, ending on a WS row and with RS facing for next row.

Back Neck and Shoulder Shaping
Sizes 142-147 cm & 152-57cm ONLY
* **Next row (RS):** Cast off 7 [8] sts, patt 15 sts on RH needle, and turn, leaving rem sts on a stitch holder.
Next row (WS): Dec 1 st at neck edge, patt to end 14 sts.
Next row: Cast off 7 sts, patt to end. 7 sts.
Next row: patt to end.
Cast off rem sts. **
With RS facing, slip next 15 sts onto a stitch holder for the centre back neck sts, rejoin yarn, K2tog, patt to end. 21 [22] sts.
Rep from * to **, reversing shapings to match first side.
All other sizes:
Cast off 5 [5: 5: 6: 7: 7: 7] sts at beg of next 2 rows. 31 [33: 35: 35: 39: 41: 43] sts.
* **Next row (RS):** Cast off 5 [5: 5: 5: 6: 6: 7] sts, patt 3 [3: 4: 4: 5: 5: 5] sts, K2tog and turn, leaving rem sts on a stitch holder. 4 [4: 5: 5: 6: 6: 6] sts.
Next row (WS): Patt to end.
Cast off rem sts. **
With RS facing, slip next 11 [13: 13: 13: 13: 15: 15] sts onto a stitch holder for the centre back neck sts, rejoin yarn, K2tog, patt to end. 9 [9: 10: 10: 12: 12: 13] sts.
Rep from * to **, reversing shapings to match first side.

LEFT FRONT
Using 10mm (US 15) needles, cast on 18 [22: 22: 26: 30: 30: 34: 34: 38] sts.
Next row (RS): * K2, P2, rep from * to last 2 sts, K2.
Next row (WS): * P2, K2, rep from * to last 2 sts, P2.
These 2 rows form rib.
Work in rib for a further 7 rows, ending on a RS row and with WS facing for next row.
Next row (WS): Keeping rib patt correct throughout, inc [dec: inc: dec: dec: inc: dec: inc: dec] 1 st at end of row. 19 [21: 23: 25: 29: 31: 33: 35: 37] sts.
With RS facing, place a stitch marker 2 [3: 4: 5: -: 1: 2: 3: 4] st(s) in from both edges. These markers will set the edge sts worked in moss st throughout.
Starting with Row 1 (RS), work edge sts and texture patt as set until work meas 29 [30: 30.5: 31: 31.5: 32: 32: 33: 33] cm from cast on, ending on a WS row and with RS facing for next row.
Armhole shaping
Next row (RS): Cast off 2 [3: 3: 4: 4: 5: 5: 6: 7] sts, patt to end. 17 [18: 20: 21: 25: 26: 28: 29: 30] sts.
Next row (WS): Patt to end.
Next row: Cast off 1 [1: 1: 1: 2: 2: 2: 3: 3] sts, patt to end. 16 [17: 19: 20: 23: 24: 26: 26: 27] sts.
Next row: Patt to end.
Next row: Cast off 1 [1: 1: 1: 1: 1: 2: 2: 2] sts, patt to end. 15 [16: 18: 19: 22: 23: 24: 24: 25] sts.
Next row: Patt to end.
Keeping patt correct throughout, dec 1 st at beg of next 1 [2: 2: 2: 2: 2: 2: 2: 2] RS rows. 14 [14: 16: 17: 20: 21: 22: 22: 23] sts.
Keeping patt correct throughout, cont working straight until work meas 22 [23: 24.5: 26: 27.5: 29: 30: 31: 32] cm from beg of armhole shaping, ending on a WS row and with RS facing for next row.

Shoulder Shaping
Next row (RS): Cast off 5 [5: 5: 6: 7: 7: 7: 7: 8] sts, patt to end. 9 [9: 11: 11: 13: 14: 15: 15: 15] sts.
Next row (WS): Patt to end.
Next row: Cast off 5 [5: 5: 5: 6: 6: 7: 7: 7] sts patt to end. 4 [4: 6: 6: 7: 8: 8: 8: 8] sts.
Next row: Patt to end.
Cast off rem sts.

RIGHT FRONT
Work as for Left Front to beg of armhole shaping, ending on a RS row and with WS facing for next row.
Armhole Shaping
Next row (WS): Cast off 2 [3: 3: 4: 4: 5: 5: 6: 7] sts, patt to end. 17 [18: 20: 21: 25: 26: 28: 29: 30] sts.
Next row (RS): Patt to end.
Next row: Cast off 1 [1: 1: 1: 2: 2: 2: 3: 3] sts, patt to end. 16 [17: 19: 20: 23: 24: 26: 26: 27] sts.
Next row: Patt to end.
Next row: Cast off 1 [1: 1: 1: 1: 1: 2: 2: 2] sts, patt to end. 15 [16: 18: 19: 22: 23: 24: 24: 25] sts.
Next row: Patt to end.
Keeping patt correct throughout, dec 1 st at beg of next 1 [2: 2: 2: 2: 2: 2: 2: 2] WS rows. 14 [14: 16: 17: 20: 21: 22: 22: 23] sts.
Keeping patt correct throughout, cont working straight until work meas 22 [23: 24.5: 26: 27.5: 29: 30: 31: 32] cm from beg of armhole shaping, ending on a RS row and with WS facing for next row.
Shoulder Shaping
Next row (WS): Cast off 5 [5: 5: 6: 7: 7: 7: 7: 8] sts, patt to end. 9 [9: 11: 11: 13: 14: 15: 15: 15] sts.
Next row (RS): Patt to end.
Next row: Cast off 5 [5: 5: 5: 6: 6: 7: 7: 7] sts, patt to end. 4 [4: 6: 6: 7: 8: 8: 8: 8] sts.
Next row: Patt to end.
Cast off rem sts.

SLEEVES
Using 10mm (US 15) needles, cast on 30 sts.
Next row (RS): * K2, P2, rep from * to last 2 sts, K2.
Next row (WS): * P2, K2, rep from * to last 2 sts, P2.
These 2 rows form rib.
Work in rib for a further 7 rows, ending on a RS row and with WS facing for next row.
Next row (WS): Keeping rib patt correct throughout, dec [dec: dec: dec: dec: inc: inc: inc: inc] 1 st at end of row. 29 [29: 29: 29: 29: 31: 31: 31: 31] sts.
With RS facing, place a st marker - [-: -: -: -: 1: 1: 1: 1] st from both edges. These markers will set the edge sts worked in moss st throughout.
Starting with Row 1 (RS), work edge sts and texture patt as set, and working increases in moss st throughout, inc 1 st at each end on every 4th [4th: 3rd: 2nd: 2nd: 2nd: 2nd: next: next] RS row 1 [6: 3: 1: 6: 9: 13: 2: 6] times, then every 5th [5th: 4th: 3rd: 3rd: 3rd: -: 2nd: 2nd] RS row 5 [1: 5: 9: 5: 3: -: 12: 9] time(s). 41 [43: 45: 49: 51: 55: 57: 59: 61] sts.
Cont working in patt without shaping until sleeve meas 45 [45: 45: 45: 43: 43: 42: 42: 41] cm from cast on, ending on a RS row and with RS facing for next row.

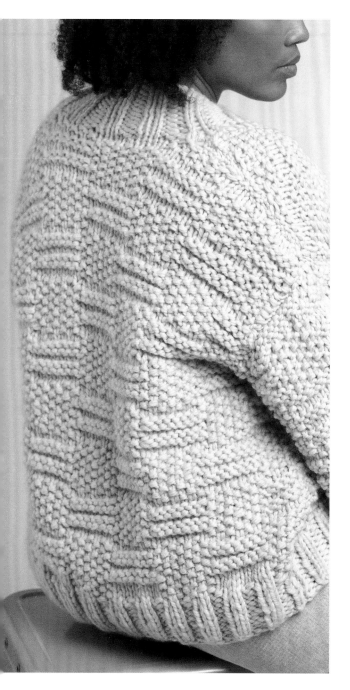

Shape top

Starting with RS facing and keeping patt correct throughout, cast off 2 [3: 3: 4: 4: 5: 5: 6: 7] sts at beg of next 2 rows, then 1 [1: 1: 1: 2: 2: 2: 3: 3] sts at beg of next 2 rows, then 1 [1: 1: 1: 1: 1: 2: 2: 2] sts at beg of next 2 rows, then dec 1 st at beg of next 2 [2: 4: 4: 4: 4: 4: 2: 4] rows. 31 [31: 29: 31: 29: 31: 31: 29: 27] sts. Cast off rem sts.

MAKING UP

Press as described on the information page.
Join both shoulder seams using back stitch, or mattress stitch if preferred.

Neckband

With RS facing, using 10mm (US 15) circular needle, beg and ending at front cast on edges, pick up and knit 53 [55: 56: 58: 60: 62: 63: 65: 66] sts up right front opening edge, 0 [0: 0: 0: 0: 0: 0: 2: 2] sts down right back neck, knit 11 [13: 13: 13: 13: 15: 15: 15: 15] sts inc [dec: inc: inc: inc: inc: dec: inc: inc: inc] 1 [1: 1: 1: 1: 1: 1: 1: 3] st from centre back neck sts on holder, pick up and knit 0 [0: 0: 0: 0: 0: 0: 2: 2] sts up left back neck, 53 [55: 56: 58: 60: 62: 63: 65: 66] sts down left front opening edge. 118 [122: 126: 130: 134: 138: 142: 150: 154] sts.
Next row (WS): * P2, K2, rep from * to last 2 sts, P2.
Next row (RS): * K2, P2, rep from * to last 2 sts, K2.
These 2 rows form rib.
Work in rib for a further 10 rows, ending on a RS row and with WS facing for next row.
Cast off loosely in rib pattern.
See information page for setting in sleeves and finishing instructions.

54 [56: 58: 60: 62: 64: 65: 67: 68] cm
21¼ [22: 22¾: 23½: 24½: 25¼: 25½: 26¼: 26¾] in

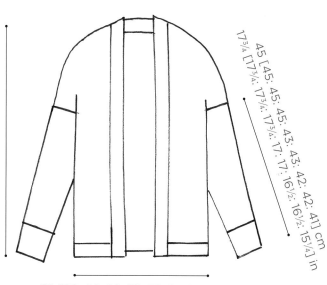

45 [45: 45: 45: 43: 43: 42: 42: 41] cm
17¾ [17¾: 17¾: 17¾: 17: 17: 16½: 16½: 15¼] in

52 [60: 62: 66: 75: 79: 83: 89: 94] cm
20¼ [22½: 24½: 26: 29½: 31: 32¾: 34¼] in

DASH

SIZE

To fit bust

71-76	81-86	91-97	102-107	112-117	122-127	132-137	142-147	152-157	cm
28-30	32-34	36-38	40-42	44-46	48-50	52-54	56-58	60-62	in

Actual bust measurement of garment

109	118	127	136	144	153	162	171	188	cm
43	46½	50¾	54¼	57¾	61¼	64¾	68¼	75¼	in

YARN

Big Wool

A – Nougat 095

7	7	8	8	9	9	10	10	11	x 100gr

B – Glum 056

4	4	5	5	5	6	6	6	7	x 100gr

NEEDLES

1 pair 10mm (no 000) (US 15) needles
10mm (no 000) (US 15) circular needle at least 120 cm long.

TENSION

9 sts and 13.5 rows to 10 cm measured over patt st
using 10mm (US 15) needles.

BACK

Using 10mm (US 15) needles and yarn B, cast on
51 [55: 59: 63: 67: 71: 75: 79: 87] sts.
Row 1 (RS): K1, *P1, K3, rep from * to last 2 sts, P1, K1.
Row 2 (WS): Purl.
Row 3: *K3, P1, rep from * to last 3 sts, K3.
Row 4: Purl.
The last 4 rows form pattern.
Continue working in set patt until work meas 40 cm
from cast on, ending on patt Row 3, with WS facing for
next row.
Break off yarn B.
Join yarn A and starting with patt row 4, continue
working in patt until work meas 82 [84: 86: 88: 90: 92:
93: 95: 96] cm, ending on a WS row and with RS facing
for next row.

Shoulder Shaping

Keeping patt correct throughout, cast off 4 [4: 4: 5: 5:
6: 6: 6: 7] sts at beg of next 12 [12: 13: 12: 12: 11: 12: 13: 12]
rows, then 1 [3: 3: 1: 3: 2: 1: -: 1] st(s) at beg of next
2 [2: 2: 2: 2: 2: -: 2] rows.
Fasten off through the rem 1 st and mark it as centre
of back neck.

LEFT FRONT

Using 10mm (US 15) needles and yarn B, cast on
23 [27: 27: 31: 31: 35: 35: 39: 43] sts.
Work as for back to beg of shoulder shaping, ending
on a WS row and with RS facing for next row.

Shoulder shaping

Keeping patt correct throughout, cast off 3 [4: 4: 5: 5: 5:
5: 6: 6] sts at beg of next 6 RS rows, then 2 [1: 1: -: -: 2: 2:
1: 3] st(s) at beg of next 2 [2: 2: -: -: 2: 2: 2: 2] RS rows.
Fasten off through the remaining 1 st and mark it for
joining to centre back neck st later.

RIGHT FRONT

Using 10mm (US 15) needles and yarn B, cast on 23 [27:
27: 31: 31: 35: 35: 39: 43] sts.
Work as for Left Front to beg of shoulder shaping,
ending on a RS row and with WS facing for next row.

Shoulder shaping

Keeping patt correct throughout, cast off 3 [4: 4: 5: 5:
5: 5: 6: 6] sts at beg of next 6 WS rows, then 2 [1: 1: -: -:
2: 2: 1: 3] st(s) at beg of next 2 [2: 2: -: -: 2: 2: 2: 2] WS
rows.
Fasten off through the remaining 1 st and mark it for
joining to centre back neck st later.

SLEEVES

Using 10mm (US 15) needles and yarn A, cast on
35 [35: 39: 39: 43: 43: 47: 51: 51] sts.
Work in patt as set for back until work measures
34 [34: 34: 34: 31: 31: 30: 30: 28] cm, ending on a WS
row and with RS facing for next row.

Sleeve shaping

Starting with a RS row and keeping patt correct
throughout, dec 1 st at each end of next 4 rows.
27 [27: 31: 31: 35: 35: 39: 43: 43] sts.
Cast off all sts.

MAKING UP

Press as described on the information page.

Join both shoulder seams using back stitch, or mattress stitch if preferred, stretching the left and right fronts slightly, so that both marked sts match up with the marked centre back neck st.

Front band

With RS facing, using 10mm (US 15) circular needle and using each yarn to match the colour changes on the garment, beg and ending at front cast on edges, pick up and knit 83 [85: 87: 89: 91: 93: 93: 95: 95] sts up right front opening edge to centre back neck, and 83 [85: 87: 89: 91: 93: 93: 95: 95] sts down left front opening edge. 166 [170: 174: 178: 182: 186: 186: 190: 190] sts.

Next row (WS): *K2, P2, rep from * to last 2 sts, K2.

The last row forms rib pattern.

Continue working in set rib patt for 6 more rows, ending on a WS row and with RS facing for next row.

Cast off loosely in rib pattern.

Mark points along side seam edges 19 [20: 21.5: 23: 24.5: 26: 27: 28: 29] cm on either side of shoulder seams to denote base of armhole openings, and join sleeves to body.

Join side and sleeve seams.

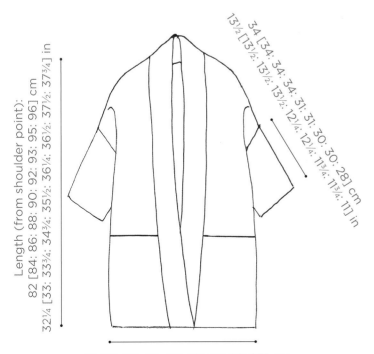

34 [34: 34: 34: 31: 31: 30: 30: 28] cm
13½ [13½: 13½: 13½: 13½: 12¼: 12¼: 11¾: 11¾: 11] in

Length (from shoulder point):
82 [84: 86: 88: 90: 92: 93: 95: 96] cm
32¼ [33: 33¾: 34¾: 35½: 36¼: 36½: 37½: 37¾] in

57 [61: 66: 70: 75: 79: 83: 88: 97] cm
22¼ [24: 25¾: 27½: 29¼: 31: 32¾: 34½: 38] in

FROTHY

SIZE
To fit bust

71-76	81-86	91-97	102-107	112-117	122-127	132-137	142-147	152-157	cm
28-30	32-34	36-38	40-42	44-46	48-50	52-54	56-58	60-62	in

Actual bust measurement of garment

100	109	118	127	140	149	158	167	180	cm
39¼	42¾	46¼	50	55	58½	62	65½	71	in

YARN
Big Wool

6	7	8	9	10	11	12	13	14	x 100g

(photographed in Floss 097)

NEEDLES
1 pair 10mm (no 000) (US 15) needles

TENSION
9 sts and 13 rows to 10 cm measured over patt st using 10mm (US 15) needles.

EXTRAS
Stitch markers
Stitch holders

Zig zag and Eyelet pattern
Row 1 (RS): Knit.
Row 2 (WS): Purl.
Row 3: *K4, P1, K3, rep from * to last st, K1.
Row 4: P1, *P2, K3, P3, rep from * to end.
Row 5: *K2, P2, K1, P2, K1, rep from * to last st, K1.
Row 6: P1, *K2, P3, K2, P1, rep from * to end.
Row 7: *P2, K5, P1, rep from * to last st, P1.
Row 8: K1, *P7, K1, rep from * to end.
Row 9: *K3, yfwd, sl 2, K1, p2sso, yfwd, K2, rep from * to last st, K1.
Row 10: Purl.
These 10 rows form zig zag and eyelet patt.

BACK
Using 10mm (US 15) needles, cast on 46 [50: 54: 58: 62: 66: 70: 78: 82] sts.
Next row (RS): * K2, P2, rep from * to last 2 sts, K2.
Next row (WS): * P2, K2, rep from * to last 2 sts, P2.
These 2 rows form rib.
Work in rib for a further 5 rows, ending on a RS row and with WS facing for next row.
Next row (WS): Keeping rib correct throughout, inc [inc: inc: inc: inc: inc: inc: dec: inc] 1 [1: 1: 1: 3: 3: 3: 1: 1] st(s) at evenly across the row. 47 [51: 55: 59: 65: 69: 73: 77: 83] sts.
With RS facing, place a stitch marker 3 [1: 3: 1: -: 2: -: 2: 1] st(s) in from both edges. These markers will set the edge sts worked in st st throughout.

Starting with row 1 (RS), work edge sts and zig zag and eyelet patt as set until work meas 32 [33: 33.5: 34: 34.5: 35: 35: 36: 36] cm from cast on, ending on a WS row and with RS facing for next row.
Shape raglan armholes
Starting with a RS row and keeping patt correct throughout, cast off 3 sts at beg of next 2 rows.
41 [45: 49: 53: 59: 63: 67: 71: 77] sts.
Starting with a RS row and keeping patt correct throughout, dec 1 st at each end of every alt row
9 [10: 10: 10: 9: 10: 9: 8: 6] times, then on every row
6 [6: 8: 10: 14: 14: 17: 20: 25] times, ending on a WS row and with RS facing for next row. 11 [13: 13: 13: 13: 15: 15: 15: 15] sts.
Break yarn and slip sts onto a holder for back neck.

FRONT
Work as for back until 8 [8: 8: 10: 10: 10: 10: 10: 12] rows less have been worked to end of raglan armhole shaping, ending on a WS row and with RS facing for next row. 25 [27: 29: 33: 33: 35: 35: 35: 39] sts.
Shape Neck
Sizes 71-76, 81-86, 91-97 cm ONLY
Next row (RS): Dec 1 st at beg, patt 5 [6: 7] sts, K2tog and turn, leaving rem sts on a stitch holder. 7 [8: 9] sts.
* **Next row (WS):** Cast off 1 [2: 3] sts at neck edge, dec 1 st at armhole edge. 5 sts.
Next row: Dec 1 st at each end. 3 sts.
Next row: Dec 1 st at armhole edge. 2 sts.
Next row: K2tog and fasten off. **

With RS facing, slip next 7 sts onto a stitch holder for centre front neck, rejoin yarn, patt 2 together, patt to last 2 sts, K2tog. 7 [8: 9] sts.
Rep from * to **, reversing shapings to match first side.

Sizes 102-107, 112-117, 122-127, 132-137, 142-147 cm ONLY

Next row (RS): Dec 1 st at beg, patt 9 sts, K2tog and turn, leaving rem sts on a stitch holder. 11 sts.
Next row (WS): Dec 1 st at each end. 9 sts.
Rep last row 3 times more. 3 sts.
Next row: Dec 1 st at armhole edge. 2 sts.
Next row: K2tog and fasten off. **
With RS facing, slip next 7 [7: 9: 9: 9] sts onto a stitch holder for centre front neck, dec 1 st at neck edge and 1 st at armhole edge. 11 sts.
Rep from * to **, reversing shapings to match first side.

Size 152-157 cm ONLY

Next row (RS): Dec 1 st at armhole edge, patt 11 sts, K2tog and turn, leaving rem sts on a stitch holder. 13 sts.
* **Next row (WS):** Dec 1 st at each end. 11 sts.
Rep last row 3 times more. 5 sts.
Next row: Dec 1 st at armhole edge. 4 sts.
Rep last row twice more. 2 sts.
Next row: K2tog and fasten off. **
With RS facing, slip next 9 sts onto a stitch holder for centre front neck, rejoin yarn, K2tog, patt to last 2 sts, dec 1 st at armhole edge. 13 sts.
Rep from * to **, reversing shapings to match first side.

SLEEVES

Using 10mm (US 15) needles, cast on 26 [26: 26: 26: 26: 30: 30: 30: 30] sts.
Next row (RS): * K2, P2, rep from * to last 2 sts, K2.
Next row (WS): * P2, K2, rep from * to last 2 sts, P2.
These 2 rows form rib.
Work in rib for a further 5 rows, ending on a RS row and with WS facing for next row.
Next row (WS): Keeping rib correct throughout, inc [inc: inc: inc: inc: dec: dec: dec: dec] 1 st at end of row. 27 [27: 27: 27: 27: 29: 29: 29: 29] sts.
With RS facing, place a stitch marker 1 [1: 1: 1: 1: 2: 2: 2: 2] st(s) in from both edges. These markers will set the edge sts worked in st st throughout.
Starting with a RS row, work in zig zag and eyelet patt with edge sts as set, inc 1 st at each end of every next [11th: 7th: 5th: 3rd: 3rd: 2nd: 2nd: 2nd] RS row 1 [1: 1: 1: 5: 1: 7: 10] time(s), then on every - [12th: 8th: 6th: 4th: 4th: 3rd: 3rd: 3rd] RS row - [1: 2: 3: 5: 2: 7: 3: 1] time(s). 29 [31: 33: 35: 39: 43: 45: 49: 51] sts.
Keeping patt correct throughout, continue working straight until work meas 44 [45: 45: 46: 46: 46: 46: 46: 46] cm from cast on, ending on a WS row and with RS facing for next row.
Shape raglan
Starting with a RS row and keeping patt correct throughout, cast off 3 sts at beg of next 2 rows. 23 [25: 27: 29: 33: 37: 39: 43: 45] sts.
Starting with a RS row and keeping patt correct throughout, dec 1 st at each end of every 4th [4th: 4th: 3rd: 3rd: 3rd: 3rd: 3rd: 3rd] row 3 [2: 1: 10: 8: 6: 5: 2: 1] time(s), then on every 3rd [3rd: 3rd: -: 2nd: 2nd: 2nd: 2nd: 2nd] row 4 [6: 8: -: 4: 8: 10: 15: 17] times, ending on a WS row and with RS facing for next row. 9 sts.

Right sleeve only

Next row (RS): Cast off 2 sts at beg and dec 1 st at end of row. 6 sts
Next row (WS): Dec 1 st at beg of row. 5 sts.
Next row: Cast off 2 sts at beg and dec 1 st at end of row. 2 sts
Cast off rem 2 sts.

Left sleeve only

Next row (RS): Dec 1 st, patt to end. 8 sts
Next row (WS): Cast off 2 sts, and dec 1 st at end of row. 5 sts.
Next row: Dec 1 st, patt to end. 4 sts.
Next row: Cast off 2 sts, patt to end. 2 sts.
Cast off rem 2 sts.

MAKING UP

Press as described on the information page.
Join both front and right back raglan seams using back stitch, or mattress stitch if preferred.

Neckband

With RS facing and using 10mm (US 15) needle, starting at left shoulder, pick up and knit 2 sts from top of sleeve cap, 4 sts down left sleeve, 5 [5: 5: 7: 7: 8: 8: 8: 9] sts down left front neck, knit 7 [7: 7: 7: 7: 9: 9: 9: 9] sts from front neck sts on holder, pick up and knit 5 [5: 5: 7: 7: 8: 8: 8: 9] sts up right front neck, 4 sts up right sleeve, 2 sts from top of sleeve cap, and knit 11 [13: 13: 13: 13: 15: 15: 15: 15] sts inc [-: -: -: -: dec: dec: dec: -] 2 [0: 0: 0: 0: 2: 2: 2: 0] sts evenly from back neck sts on holder.
42 [42: 42: 46: 46: 50: 50: 50: 54] sts.
Next row (WS): * P2, K2, rep from * to last 2 sts, P2.
Next row (RS): * K2, P2, rep from * to last 2 sts, K2.
These 2 rows form rib.
Work in rib for a further 2 rows, ending on a RS row and with WS facing for next row.
Cast off in rib.
Join left back and neck seams.
Join sleeves and side seams using back stitch, or mattress stitch if preferred.

52 [54: 56: 58: 60: 62: 63: 65: 66] cm
20½ [21¼: 22: 22½: 23½: 24½: 24¾: 25½: 26] in

44 [45: 45: 46: 46: 46: 46: 46: 46] cm
17¼ [17¾: 17¾: 18: 18: 18: 18: 18: 18] in
Sleeves (at underarm):

52 [57: 61: 66: 72: 77: 81: 86: 92] cm
20½ [22¼: 24: 25¾: 28½: 30: 32: 33¾: 36¼] in

MELLOW

SIZE
To fit bust

71-76	81-86	91-97	102-107	112-117	122-127	132-137	142-147	152-157	cm
28-30	32-34	36-38	40-42	44-46	48-50	52-54	56-58	60-62	in

Actual bust measurement of garment

87	100	109	118	127	140	149	158	171	cm
33¼	38½	42	45½	49	54¼	57¾	61¼	66½	in

YARN
Big Wool
A Limeade 096 / Floss 097

5	5	6	6	6	7	7	7	7	x 100gr

B Nougat 095 / Melon 094

3	3	4	4	5	5	6	6	6	x 100gr

NEEDLES
1 pair 10mm (no 000) (US 15) needles

TENSION
9 sts and 12.5 rows to 10 cm measured over st st using 10mm (US 15) needles.

EXTRAS
Stitch holders

BACK
Using 10mm (US 15) needles and yarn A, cast on 38 [46: 50: 54: 58: 62: 66: 70: 78] sts.
Next row (RS): * K2, P2, rep from * to last 2 sts, K2.
Next row (WS): * P2, K2, rep from * to last 2 sts, P2.
These 2 rows form rib.
Work in rib for a further 3 rows, ending on a RS row and with WS facing for next row.
Next row (WS): Keeping rib patt correct throughout, inc 1 [0: 0: 0: 0: 1: 1: 1: 0] st at each end.
40 [46: 50: 54: 58: 64: 68: 72: 78] sts.
Starting with a K row, work in st st, changing to yarn B on a RS row after 12 rows have been completed, then changing yarns every 12 rows, until work meas 42 [43: 43.5: 44: 44.5: 45: 45: 46: 46] cm from cast on.

Armhole Shaping
Continuing working in st st and keeping stripe pattern as set throughout, cast off 1 [2: 2: 3: 4: 5: 6: 7: 7] sts at beg of next 2 rows, then 1 [1: 1: 1: 1: 1: 1: 1: 3] sts at beg of next 2 rows, then dec 1 st at each end of next 0 [1: 2: 2: 2: 2: 2: 2: 2] RS rows. 36 [38: 40: 42: 44: 48: 50: 52: 54] sts.
Continue working straight in patt until work meas 19 [20: 21.5: 23: 24.5: 26: 27: 28: 29] cm from beg of armhole shaping, ending on a WS row and with RS facing for next row.
Note: Do not change colour after the 7th stripe in yarn A, continue working in Yarn A to end of shoulder shaping.

Back Neck and Shoulder Shaping
Starting on a RS row and working in st st throughout, cast off 4 [4: 4: 5: 5: 5: 6: 6: 6] sts at beg of next 2 rows. 28 [30: 32: 32: 34: 38: 38: 40: 42] sts.
Sizes 102-107, 112-117, 122-127, 132-137, 142-147, 152-157 cm ONLY
Next row (RS): Cast off 4 [5: 5: 5: 6: 6] sts, K 3 [3: 4: 4: 5: 6], K2tog and turn, leaving rem sts on a stitch holder. 4 [4: 5: 5: 6: 7] sts.
Next row (WS): Dec 0 [0: 0: 0: 1: 1] st at neck edge, P to end. 4 [4: 5: 5: 5: 6] sts.
Cast off rem sts.
With RS facing, slip next 14 [14: 16: 16: 14: 14] sts on a stitch holder for centre back neck sts, rejoin yarn, K2tog, K to end. 8 [9: 10: 10: 12: 13] sts.
Next row (WS): Cast off 4 [5: 5: 5: 6: 6] sts, P to end. 4 [4: 5: 5: 6: 7].
Next row: Dec 0 [0: 0: 0: 1: 1] st at neck edge, K to end. 4 [4: 5: 5: 5: 6] sts.
Cast off rem sts.
Sizes 71-76, 81-86, 91-97 cm ONLY
Next row (RS): Cast off 4 sts, K 3 [3: 4] sts and turn, leaving rem sts on a stitch holder. 7 [7: 8] sts.
Next row (WS): Purl.
Cast off rem sts.
With RS facing, slip next 14 [16: 16] sts onto a stitch holder for centre back neck sts, rejoin yarn and K to end. 7 [7: 8] sts.
Next row (WS): Cast off 4 sts, P to end. 3 [3: 4] sts.
Next row: Knit.
Cast off rem sts.

FRONT

Work as for Back until 8 rows less have been worked to start of shoulder shaping, ending on a WS row and with RS facing for next row.

Left Front Neck Shaping

Next row (RS): K 14 [14: 15: 16: 17: 18: 19: 20: 21] sts and turn, leaving rem sts on a stitch holder.

Next row (WS): Purl.

Next row: K to last 3 sts, K2tog, K1. 13 [13: 14: 15: 16: 17: 18: 19: 20] sts.

Repeat the last 2 rows twice more. 11 [11: 12: 13: 14: 15: 16: 17: 18] sts.

Starting with a purl row, continue working in st st until work meas 19 [20: 21.5: 23: 24.5: 26: 27: 28: 29] cm from beg of armhole shaping, ending on a WS row and with RS facing for next row.

Note: Do not change colour after the 7th stripe in yarn A, continue working in Yarn A to end of shoulder shaping.

Left Front Shoulder Shaping

Next row (RS): Cast off 4 [4: 4: 5: 5: 5: 6: 6: 6] sts and K to end. 7 [7: 8: 8: 9: 10: 10: 11: 12] sts.

Next row (WS): Purl.

Next row: Cast off 4 [4: 4: 4: 5: 5: 5: 6] sts, K to end. 3 [3: 4: 4: 4: 5: 5: 5: 6] sts.

Next row: Purl to end.

Cast off rem sts.

Right Front

With RS facing, slip next 8 [10: 10: 10: 10: 12: 12: 12: 12] sts onto a stitch holder for centre front neck sts, rejoin yarn and K to end. 14 [14: 15: 16: 17: 18: 19: 20: 21] sts.

Complete to match first side, reversing shapings.

SLEEVES

Using 10mm (US 15) needles and yarn A, cast on 26 sts.

Next row (RS): * K2, P2, rep from * to last 2 sts, K2.

Next row (WS): * P2, K2, rep from * to last 2 sts, P2.

These 2 rows form rib.

Work in rib for a further 3 rows, ending on a RS row and with WS facing for next row.

Next row (WS): Keeping rib patt correct throughout, inc 0 [0: 0: 1: 1: 1: 1: 1: 1] sts at each end of row. 26 [26: 26: 28: 28: 28: 28: 28: 28] sts.

Starting with a Knit row, work in st st throughout, changing yarns every 12 rows (10 cm - starting from beg of work, so that stripes match with Front and Back) as set stripe pattern, inc 1 st at each end of every 6th [4th: 4th: 4th: 2nd: 2nd: 2nd: next: next] RS row 4 [1: 6: 6: 1: 4: 9: 1: 4] time(s), then every - [5th: -: -: 3rd: 3rd: 3rd: 2nd: 2nd] RS row - [4: -: -: 7: 5: 1: 10: 8] times. 34 [36: 38: 40: 44: 46: 48: 50: 52] sts.

Continue working straight in st st until work meas 48 [48: 48: 48: 46: 46: 44: 44: 42] cm from beg, ending on a WS row and with RS facing for next row.

Sleeve Cap

Continuing working in st st and keeping stripe pattern as set throughout, cast off 1 [2: 2: 3: 4: 5: 6: 7: 7] sts at beg of next 2 rows, then 1 [1: 1: 1: 1: 1: 1: 1: 3] sts at beg of next 2 rows, then dec 1 st at each end of next 0 [1: 2: 2: 2: 2: 2: 2: 2] RS rows. 30 [28: 28: 28: 30: 30: 30: 30: 28] sts.

Cast off rem sts.

MAKING UP

Press as described on the information page.

Join right shoulder seam using back stitch, or mattress stitch if preferred.

Neckband

With RS facing, using 10mm (US 15) needle and yarn A, beg at left shoulder, pick up and knit 8 [8: 8: 9: 9: 10: 10: 10: 10] sts down left neck edge, knit 8 [10: 10: 10: 10: 12: 12: 12: 12] sts from centre front neck sts on holder, pick up and knit 8 [8: 8: 9: 9: 10: 10: 10: 10] sts up right neck edge, 0 [0: 0: 1: 1: 1: 1: 2: 2] sts down right back neck, knit 14 [16: 16: 14: 14: 16: 16: 14: 14] sts and evenly -: [-: -: -: inc: inc: -: dec: -: -] 0 [0: 0: 2: 2: 0: 2: 0: 0] sts from centre back neck sts on holder, pick up and knit 0 [0: 0: 1: 1: 1: 1: 2: 2] sts up left back neck. 38 [42: 42: 46: 46: 50: 50: 50: 50] sts.

Next row (RS): * K2, P2, rep from * to last 2 sts, K2.

Next row (WS): * P2, K2, rep from * to last 2 sts, P2.

These 2 rows form rib.

Work in rib for a further 28 rows, ending on a RS row and with WS facing for next row.

Cast off loosely in rib pattern.

Join left shoulder and neckband seam.

See information page for setting in sleeves and finishing instructions.

64 [66: 68: 70: 72: 74: 75: 77: 78] cm
25¼ [26: 26¾: 27½: 28¼: 29¼: 29½: 30¼: 30¾] in

48 [48: 48: 48: 46: 44: 44: 42] cm
19 [19: 19: 19: 18: 18: 17¼: 17½: 16½] in
Sleeves (at underarm):

44 [51: 56: 60: 64: 71: 76: 80: 87] cm
17½ [20: 21¾: 23½: 25½: 28: 29¾: 31½: 34] in

SWISH

SIZE
Approx 34 cm (13¼ in) wide and 230 cm (90½ in) long.

YARN
Big Wool
8 x 100gm
(photographed in Melon 094)

NEEDLES
1 pair 10mm (no 000) (US 15) needles

TENSION
14 sts and 13 rows to 10 cm measured over patt st using 10mm (US 15) needles.

EXTRAS
Cable needle

ABBREVIATIONS
Cr11: Slip next 5 sts onto a cable needle and hold in front of the work, (K2, P1) twice from left-hand needle, then K2, P1, K2 from cable needle.

SCARF
Using 10mm (US 15) needle, cast on 47 sts.
Row 1 (RS): K2, *P1, K2, rep from * to end.
Row 2 (WS): P2, *K1, P2, rep from * to end.
Row 3: As row 1.
Row 4: As row 2.
Row 5: (K2, P1) twice, Cr11, (P1, K2) 4 times, P1, Cr11, (P1, K2) twice.
Row 6: As row 2.
Row 7: As row 1.
Row 8: As row 2.
Row 9: As row 1.
Row 10: As row 2.
Rows 10-20: As rows 1-10
Row 21: As row 1.
Row 22: As row 2.
Row 23: As row 1.
Row 24: As row 2.
Row 25: (K2, P1) 6 times, Cr11, (P1, K2) 6 times.
Row 26: As row 2.
Row 27: As row 1.
Row 28: As row 2.
Row 29: As row 1.
Row 30: As row 2.
Rows 31-40: As rows 21-30.
These 40 rows form patt.
Rep rows 1-40 a further 6 times, then rep rows 1-19 once more, ending on a RS row and with WS facing for next row.
Cast off loosely.

MAKING UP
Press as described on the information page.

WHISPER

SIZE
To fit bust

71-76	81-86	91-97	102-107	112-117	122-127	132-137	142-147	152-157	cm
28-30	32-34	36-38	40-42	44-46	48-50	52-54	56-58	60-62	in

Actual bust measurement of garment

109	120	127	128	149	156	171	178	193	cm
43	47¼	50	54½	58¾	61½	67¼	70¼	76	in

YARN
Big Wool

11	12	13	13	14	15	16	17	18	x 100gr

(photographed in White Hot 001)

NEEDLES
1 pair 10mm (no 000) (US 15) needles
10mm (no 000) (US 15) circular needle at least 120 cm long

TENSION
11 sts and 14 rows to 10 cm measured over patt st
using 10mm (US 15) needles.

EXTRAS
Stitch markers
Stitch holder

Lace Mock Cable Pattern
Row 1 (RS): *P2, K6, rep from * to last 2 sts, P2.
Row 2 and every WS row: *K2, P6, rep from * to last 2 sts, K2.
Row 3: *P2, yon, K2, sl1K, K1, psso, K2, rep from * to last 2 sts, P2.
Row 5: *P2, K1, yfwd, K2, sl1, K1, psso, K1, rep from * to last 2 sts, P2.
Row 7: *P2, K2, yfwd, K2, sl1, K1, psso, rep from * to last 2 sts, P2.
Row 9: As Row 1.
Row 11: *P2, K2, K2tog, K2, yfrn, rep from * to last 2 sts, P2.
Row 13: *P2, K1, K2tog, K2, yfwd, K1, rep from * to last 2 sts, P2.
Row 15: *P2, K2tog, K2, yfwd, K2, rep from * to last 2 sts, P2.
Row 16: as Row 2.
The last 16 rows form the Lace Mock Cable Pattern.
Repeat rows 1-16 throughout.

BACK
Using 10mm (US 15) needles, cast on 62 [66: 70: 78: 82: 86: 94: 98: 106] sts.
Next row (RS): *K2, P2, rep from * to last 2 sts, K2.
Next row (WS): * P2, K2, rep from * to last 2 sts, P2.
These 2 rows form rib.
Work in rib for a further 7 rows, ending on a RS row and with WS facing for next row.

Next row (WS): Keeping rib correct throughout,
- [inc: inc: -: inc: inc: inc: inc: inc] 1 st at each end.
62 [68: 72: 78: 84: 88: 96: 100: 108] sts.
With RS facing, place a stitch marker 2 [1: 3: 2: 1: 3: 3: 1: 1] st(s) in from both edges. These markers will set the edge sts worked in rev st st throughout.
Starting with Row 1 (RS), work edge sts and lace mock cable patt as set until work meas 52 [53: 53: 54: 54: 55: 55: 56: 56] cm from cast on, ending on a WS row and with RS facing for next row.

Armhole Shaping
Starting with RS facing and keeping patt correct throughout, cast off 3 [4: 4: 5: 6: 6: 7: 8: 9] sts at beg of next 2 rows, then 1 [2: 2: 2: 2: 2: 3: 3: 4] sts at beg of next 2 rows, then 1 [1: 1: 1: 2: 2: 2: 2: 3] sts at beg of next 2 rows, then 0 [0: 1: 1: 1: 1: 2: 2: 2] sts at beg of next 2 rows. 52 [54: 56: 60: 62: 66: 68: 70: 72] sts.
Keeping patt correct throughout, continue working straight until work meas 19 [20: 21.5: 23: 24.5: 26: 27: 28: 29] cm from beg of armhole shaping, ending on a WS row and with RS facing for next row.

Back neck and Shoulder Shaping
Sizes 142-147 cm & 152-57cm ONLY
Next row (RS): Cast off 9 [9] sts, patt 16 [17] sts on RH needle, K2tog and turn, leaving rem sts on a stitch holder. 17 [18] sts.
* Next row (WS): Dec 1 st at neck edge, patt to end. 16 [17] sts
Next row: Cast off 8 [9] sts, patt to end. 8 [8] sts.

Next row: Patt to end.
Cast off all sts.**
With RS facing, slip next 16 [16] sts onto a stitch holder for centre back neck sts, rejoin yarn to the rem sts, K2tog and patt to end. 20 [27] sts
Next row (WS): Cast off 9 [9] sts, patt to end. 17 [18] sts.
Repeat from * to **, reversing shapings to match first side.

All other sizes:
Cast off 6 [7: 7: 7: 8: 8: 8] sts at beg of next 2 rows. 40 [40: 42: 46: 46: 50: 52] sts.
Next row (RS): Cast off 6 [6: 7: 7: 7: 8: 8] sts, patt 6 [6: 6: 7: 7: 7: 8] sts on RH needle, K2tog and turn, leaving rem sts on a stitch holder. 7 [7: 7: 8: 8: 8: 9] sts.
* **Next row (WS):** Dec 1 st at neck edge, patt to end.
6 [6: 6: 7: 7: 7: 8] sts.
Cast off all sts.**
With RS facing, slip next 12 [12: 12: 14: 14: 16: 16] sts onto a stitch holder for centre back neck sts, rejoin yarn to the rem sts, K2tog and patt to end. 13 [13: 14: 15: 15: 16: 17] sts.
Next row (WS): Cast off 6 [6: 7: 7: 7: 8: 8] sts, patt to end. 7 [7: 7: 8: 8: 8: 9] sts.
Repeat from * to **, reversing shapings to match first side.

LEFT FRONT

Using 10mm (US 15) needles, cast on 22 [26: 26: 30: 34: 34: 38: 42: 42] sts.
Next row (RS): *K2, P2, rep from * to last 2 sts, K2.
Next row (WS): * P2, K2, rep from * to last 2 sts, P2.
These 2 rows form rib.
Work in rib for a further 7 rows, ending on a RS row and with WS facing for next row.
Next row (WS): Keeping rib correct throughout, - [-: inc: -: -: inc: -: -: inc] 1 st at each end. 22 [26: 28: 30: 34: 36: 38: 42: 44] sts.
With RS facing, place a st marker 2 [-: 1: 2: -: 1: 2: -: 1] st(s) from both edges. These markers will set the edge sts worked in rev st st throughout.
Starting with Row 1 (RS), work edge sts and lace mock cable patt as set until work meas 55 [56: 56.5: 57: 57.5: 58: 58: 59: 59] cm from beg, ending on a WS row and with RS facing for next row.

Armhole Shaping
Next row (RS): Cast off 3 [4: 4: 5: 6: 7: 7: 8: 9] sts, patt to end. 19 [22: 24: 25: 28: 29: 31: 34: 35] sts.
Next row (WS): Patt to end.
Next row: Cast off 1 [2: 2: 2: 2: 3: 3: 3: 4] sts, patt to end. 18 [20: 22: 23: 26: 26: 28: 31: 31] sts.
Next row: Patt to end.
Next row: Cast off 1 [1: 1: 1: 2: 2: 2: 3: 3] sts, patt to end. 17 [19: 21: 22: 24: 24: 26: 28: 28] sts.
Next row: Patt to end.
Next row: Cast off 0 [0: 1: 1: 1: 1: 2: 3: 2] sts, patt to end. 17 [19: 20: 21: 23: 23: 24: 25: 26] sts.
Keeping patt correct throughout, continue working straight until work meas 16 [17: 18.5: 20: 21.5: 23: 24: 25: 26] cm from beg of armhole shaping, ending on a WS row and with RS facing for next row.

Shoulder Shaping
Next row (RS): Cast off 6 [7: 7: 7: 8: 8: 8: 9: 9] sts, patt to end. 11 [12: 13: 14: 15: 15: 16: 16: 17] sts.
Next row (WS): Patt to end.
Next row: Cast off 6 [6: 7: 7: 7: 8: 8: 8: 9] sts, patt to end. 5 [6: 6: 7: 8: 7: 8: 8: 8] sts.
Next row: Patt to end.
Cast off rem sts.

RIGHT FRONT

Work as for Left Front until beg of armhole shaping, ending on a RS row and with WS facing for next row.

Armhole Shaping
Next row (WS): Cast off 3 [4: 4: 5: 6: 7: 7: 8: 9] sts, patt to end. 19 [22: 24: 25: 28: 29: 31: 34: 35] sts.
Next row (RS): Patt to end.
Next row: Cast off 1 [2: 2: 2: 2: 3: 3: 3: 4] sts, patt to end. 18 [20: 22: 23: 26: 26: 28: 31: 31] sts.
Next row: Patt to end.
Next row: Cast off 1 [1: 1: 1: 2: 2: 2: 3: 3] sts, patt to end. 17 [19: 21: 22: 24: 24: 26: 28: 28] sts.
Next row: Patt to end.
Next row: Cast off 0 [0: 1: 1: 1: 2: 3: 2] sts, patt to end. 17 [19: 20: 21: 23: 23: 24: 25: 26] sts.
Keeping patt correct throughout, continue working straight until work meas 16 [17: 18.5: 20: 21.5: 23: 24: 25: 26] cm from beg of armhole shaping, ending on a RS row and with WS facing for next row.

Shoulder Shaping
Next row (WS): Cast off 6 [7: 7: 7: 8: 8: 8: 9: 9] sts, patt to end. 11 [12: 13: 14: 15: 15: 16: 16: 17] sts.
Next row (RS): Patt to end.
Next row: Cast off 6 [6: 7: 7: 7: 8: 8: 8: 9] sts, patt to end. 5 [6: 6: 7: 8: 7: 8: 8: 8] sts.
Next row: Patt to end.
Cast off rem sts.

SLEEVES

Using 10mm (US 15) needles, cast on 30 [30: 30: 30: 30: 30: 30: 34: 34] sts.
Next row (RS): *K2, P2, rep from * to last 2 sts, K2.
Next row (WS): * P2, K2, rep from * to last 2 sts, P2.
These 2 rows form rib.
Work in rib for a further 7 rows, ending on a RS row and with WS facing for next row.
Next row (WS): Keeping rib correct throughout, - [-: inc: inc: inc: inc: inc: -: -] 1 st at each end. 30 [30: 32: 32: 32: 32: 32: 34: 34] sts.
With RS facing, place a st marker 2 [2: 3: 3: 3: 3: 3: -: -] st(s) from both edges. These markers will set the edge sts worked in rev st st throughout.
Starting with Row 1 (RS), work edge sts and lace mock cable patt as set, and working increases in rev st st throughout, inc 1 st at each end on every 4th [3rd: 3rd: 2nd: 2nd: next: next: next: next] RS row 2 [5: 5: 4: 9: 3: 6: 6: 9] times, then every 5th [4th: 4th: 3rd: 3rd: 2nd: 2nd: 2nd: 2nd] RS row 3 [2: 2: 5: 1: 9: 7: 7: 5] time(s). 40 [44: 46: 50: 52: 56: 58: 60: 62] sts.
Continue working in patt without shaping until sleeve meas 45 [45: 45: 45: 42: 42: 41: 41: 39] cm from cast on, ending on a RS row and with RS facing for next row.

Shape top
Starting with RS facing and keeping patt correct throughout, cast off 3 [4: 4: 5: 6: 6: 7: 8: 9] sts at beg of next 2 rows, then 1 [2: 2: 2: 2: 2: 3: 3: 4] sts at beg of next 2 rows, then 1 [1: 1: 1: 2: 2: 2: 2: 3] sts at beg of next 2 rows, then 0 [0: 1: 1: 1: 1: 2: 2: 2] sts at beg of next 2 rows. 30 [30: 30: 32: 30: 34: 30: 30: 26] sts.
Cast off rem sts.

MAKING UP
Press as described on the information page.
Join both shoulder seams using back stitch, or mattress stitch if preferred.

Neckband
With RS facing, using 10mm (US 15) circular needle, beg and ending at front cast on edges, pick up and knit 83 [85: 87: 90: 92: 93: 95: 97: 99] sts up right front opening edge, 0 [0: 0: 0: 0: 0: 0: 2: 2] sts down right back neck, knit 12 [12: 12: 14: 14: 16: 16: 16: 16] sts from centre back neck sts on holder, pick up and knit 0 [0: 0: 0: 0: 0: 0: 2: 2] sts up left back neck, 83 [85: 87: 90: 92: 93: 95: 97: 99] sts down left front opening edge. 178 [182: 186: 194: 198: 202: 206: 214: 218] sts.

Next row (WS): *K2, P2, rep from * to last 2 sts, K2.
The last row forms rib pattern.
Continue working in set rib patt for 7 more rows, ending on a RS row and with WS facing for next row.
Cast off loosely in rib pattern.

Belt
Using 10mm (US 15) needle, cast on 7 sts.
Row 1 (RS): K2 *P1, K1, rep from * to last st, K1.
Row 2 (WS): K1, *P1, K1, rep from * to end.
These 2 rows form rib.
Continue working in patt until work meas 140 cm from beg, ending on a RS row and with WS facing for next row.
Cast off in rib
See information page for setting in sleeves and finishing instructions.
Pattern note: sizes 112 - 127 & 142 - 147 only will have 1 stitch difference on 2 cast off rows. Sleeve should be eased into this difference.

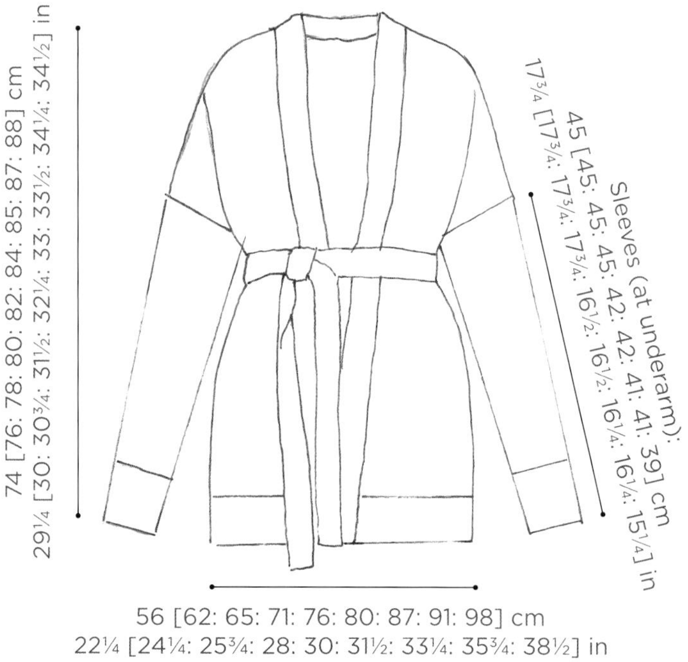
74 [76: 78: 80: 82: 84: 85: 87: 88] cm
29¼ [30: 30¾: 31½: 32¼: 33: 33½: 34¼: 34½] in
Sleeves (at underarm):
45 [45: 45: 45: 42: 42: 41: 41: 39] cm
17¾ [17¾: 17¾: 17¾: 16½: 16½: 16¼: 16¼: 15¼] in
56 [62: 65: 71: 76: 80: 87: 91: 98] cm
22¼ [24¼: 25¾: 28: 30: 31½: 33¼: 35¾: 38½] in

WHOOSH

SIZE
Approx 36 cm (14 in) wide and 230 cm (90½ in) long.

YARN
Big Wool
5 x 100gm
photographed in White Hot 001)

NEEDLES
1 pair 10mm (no 000) (US 15) needles

TENSION
10 sts and 13.5 rows to 10 cm measured over patt st
using 10mm (US 15) needles.

SCARF
Using 10mm (US 15) needle, cast on 36 sts.
Row 1 (RS): *K2tog, (yfwd) twice, K2tog, rep from *
to end.
Row 2 (WS): *P1, (K1, P1) into double yfwd of previous
row, P1, rep from * to end.
Row 3: K2, *sl 1, K1, psso, (yfwd) twice, sl 1, K1, psso,
rep from * to last 2 sts, K2.
Row 4: P2, *P1, (K1, P1) into double yfwd of previous
row, P1, rep from * to last 2 sts, P2.
These 4 rows form patt.
Rep the last 4 rows a further 76 times, (work should
meas approx 228cm) ending on a WS row and with
RS facing for next row.
Cast off loosely.

MAKING UP
Press as described on the information page.

ZAP

○ ● ●

SIZE
To fit bust

71-76	81-86	91-97	102-107	112-117	122-127	132-137	142-147	152-157	cm
28-30	32-34	36-38	40-42	44-46	48-50	52-54	56-58	60-62	in

Actual bust measurement of garment

76	88	100	112	118	130	136	148	160	cm
30	34¾	39¼	44	46½	51¼	53½	58¼	63	in

YARNS
Big Wool
Short Version

3	4	4	5	5	6	6	7	7	x 100gm

(photographed in Limeade 096)

Long Version

4	4	5	6	6	7	7	8	8	x 100gm

(photographed in Concrete 061)

NEEDLES
1 pair 10mm (no 000) (US 15) needles
1 pair 9mm (no 00) (US 13) needles

TENSION
10 sts and 14 rows to 10 cm measured over patt st
using 10mm (US 15) needles.

EXTRAS
Stitch holders
Stitch markers

BACK
Using 10mm (US 15) needles, cast on 42 [46: 50: 58: 62:
66: 70: 74: 82] sts.
Next row (RS): *K2, P2, rep from * to last 2 sts, K2.
Next row (WS): * P2, K2, rep from * to last 2 sts, P2.
These 2 rows form rib.
Work in rib for a further 5 rows, ending on a RS row and
with WS facing for next row.
Next row (WS): Keeping rib patt correct throughout,
dec [-: inc: -: dec: inc: -: inc: -] 2 [0: 2: 0: 1: 1:
0: 2: 0] st(s) evenly across the row. 40 [46: 52: 58: 61:
67: 70: 76: 82] sts.
Next row (RS): P3, *K1, P2, rep from * to last st, P1.
Next row (WS): K3, *wyif, sl 1 purlwise, wyib, K2, rep
from * to last st, K1.
The last 2 rows form the slipped-stitch rib pattern.
Continue working in slipped-stitch rib patt as set until
work meas 13 [14: 14: 15: 15: 16: 16: 17: 17] cm from cast
on (Short Version), or 31 [32: 32: 33: 33: 34:
34: 35: 35] cm from cast on (Long Version), ending on
a WS row and with RS facing for next row.
Armhole Shaping
Starting with a RS row and keeping pattern as set
throughout, cast off 1 [2: 2: 2: 2: 3: 3: 4: 4] sts at beg of
next 2 rows, then 1 [1: 1: 2: 2: 3: 3: 3: 4] sts at beg of next
2 rows, then 0 [0: 1: 1: 2: 2: 2: 3: 4] at beg of next 2 rows.
36 [40: 44: 48: 49: 51: 54: 56: 58] sts.

Continue working straight in patt until work meas
19 [20: 21.5: 23: 24.5: 26: 27: 28: 29] cm from beg of
armhole shaping, ending on a WS row and with RS
facing for next row.
Shoulder Shaping
Starting with a RS row and keeping pattern as set
throughout, cast off 2 [2: 3: 4: 4: 4: 4: 3: 4] sts at beg
of next 2 rows, then 2 [2: 3: 3: 3: 3: 3: 3: 3] sts at beg of
next 2 rows, then 2 [2: 2: 2: 3: 3: 3: 3: 3] at beg of next
2 rows. 24 [28: 28: 30: 29: 31: 34: 38: 38] sts.
Back Neck and Shoulder Shaping
Sizes 142-147, 152-157 cm ONLY
Next row (RS): Cast off 3 sts, patt 6 sts on RH needle,
K2tog and turn, leaving rem sts on a stitch holder. 7 sts
* **Next row (WS):** Dec 1 st at neck edge, patt to end. 6 sts.
Next row: Cast off 3 sts, patt to end. 3 sts.
Next row: Patt to end.
Cast off rem sts. **
With RS facing, slip next 16 sts on a stitch holder for
centre back neck sts, rejoin yarn, K2tog and patt
to end. 10 sts.
Next row (WS): Cast off 3 sts, patt to end. 7 sts.
Rep from * to **, reversing shapings to match first side.

All other sizes

Starting with a RS row and keeping patt correct throughout, cast off 2 [2: 2: 2: 2: 2: 3] sts at beg of next 2 rows. 20 [24: 24: 26: 25: 27: 28] sts.

Next row (RS): Cast off 1 [2: 2: 2: 2: 2: 2] sts, patt 1 [2: 2: 2: 2: 3: 3] sts on RH needle and turn, leaving rem sts on a stitch holder.

* **Next row (WS):** Dec 0 [0: 0: 1: 1: 1: 1] st at neck edge, patt to end. 1 [2: 2: 2: 2: 2: 2] sts.

Next row: Patt to end.

Cast off rem sts. **

With RS facing, slip next 16 [16: 16: 16: 15: 17: 18] sts, rejoin yarn and patt to end. 2 [4: 4: 5: 5: 5: 5] sts.

Next row (WS): Cast off 1 [2: 2: 2: 2: 2: 2] sts, patt to end. 1 [2: 2: 3: 3: 3: 3] sts.

Cast off rem sts.

Rep from * to **, reversing shapings to match first side.

FRONT

Work as for Back until work meas 17 [18: 20: 21: 23: 24: 25: 27: 27] cm from beg (Short Version) or 35 [36: 38: 39: 41: 42: 43: 45: 45] cm from beg (Long Version), ending on a RS row and with WS facing for next row.

Next row (WS): Keeping patt correct throughout, dec [dec: dec: dec: -: -: inc: inc: inc] 1 st at beg of row. 35 [39: 43: 47: 49: 51: 55: 57: 59] sts.

Left Front Neck Shaping

Next row (RS): Patt 17 [19: 21: 23: 24: 25: 27: 28: 29] sts and turn, leaving rem sts on a stitch holder.

* **Next row (WS):** Patt to end.

Starting with a RS row and keeping patt correct throughout, dec 1 st at neck edge of next and every 2nd [2nd: 2nd: next: next: next: next: next: next] RS row 6 [6: 6: 1: 1: 3: 4: 5: 5] times, then on every - [-: -: 2nd: 2nd: 2nd: next: next: next] RS row - [-: -: 6: 6: 5: 5: 4: 4] times,

AND AT THE SAME TIME start shaping the shoulders on RS rows when work meas 19 [20: 21.5: 23: 24.5: 26: 27: 28: 29] cm from beg of armhole shaping as follows:

Cast off 2 [2: 3: 4: 4: 4: 4: 3: 4] sts at armhole edge on next RS row, then cast off 2 [2: 3: 3: 3: 3: 3: 3: 3] sts at beg of next RS row, then cast off 2 [2: 2: 2: 3: 3: 3: 3: 3] sts at beg of next RS row, then cast off 2 [2: 2: 2: 2: 3: 3: 3] sts at beg of next RS row, then cast off 1 [2: 2: 2: 2: 2: 2: 3: 3] sts at beg of next 2 RS rows. **

Cast off rem sts.

Right Front Neck Shaping

With RS facing, slip next st onto a stitch holder for centre front neck st, patt to end. 17 [19: 21: 23: 24: 25: 27: 28: 29] sts.

Rep from * to **, reversing shapings to match first side.

MAKING UP

Press as described on the information page.

Join right shoulder seam using back stitch, or mattress stitch if preferred.

Neckband

With RS facing, using 9mm (US 13) needle, beg at left shoulder, rejoin yarn and pick up and knit 22 [22: 22: 22: 22: 26: 26: 26: 26] sts down left neck edge, place a stitch marker, knit centre front neck st on holder, place a stitch marker, pick up and knit 22 [22: 22: 22: 22: 26: 26: 26: 26] sts up right neck edge, 2 [2: 2: 2: 2: 2: 1: 3: 3] sts

down right back neck, knit 16 [16: 17: 16: 15: 17: 18: 16: 16] sts - [-: dec: -: inc: dec: inc: inc: inc] 0 [0: 1: 0: 1: 2: 2: 2] st(s) evenly across centre back neck sts on holder, pick up and knit 2 [2: 2: 2: 2: 2: 3: 3] sts up left back neck. 65 [65: 65: 65: 65: 73: 77: 77: 77] sts.

Next row (WS): (K2, P2) until 2 sts before first marker, K2, slip marker, purl centre st, slip marker, (K2, P2) to last 2 sts, K2.

Next row (RS): Keeping rib patt correct and centre st worked in st st throughout, dec 1 st on either side of centre st, slipping markers from left to right needle as they present. 59 [59: 59: 63: 63: 71: 71: 75: 75] sts.

Next row: Patt to centre st, purl centre st, patt to end. Work 1 more RS dec row. 57 [57: 57: 61: 61: 69: 69: 73: 73] sts.

Cast off in pattern.

Join left shoulder and neckband seam.

Armband

With RS facing, using 9mm (US 13) needle and starting at bottom of left armhole, pick up and knit 38 [42: 46: 54: 62: 66: 70: 74: 82] sts evenly along armhole edge.

Next row (WS): * P2, K2, rep from * to last 2 sts, P2.

Next row (RS): *K2, P2, rep from * to last 2 sts, K2. These 2 rows form rib.

Work in rib for a further 2 rows, ending on a RS row and with WS facing for next row.

Cast off in pattern.

Sew armhole seam and join side seams using mattress stitch.

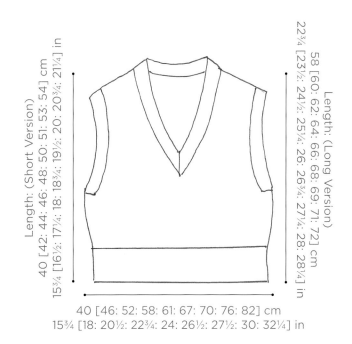

Length: (Short Version)
40 [42: 44: 46: 48: 50: 51: 53: 54] cm
15¾ [16½: 16½: 17¼: 18: 18¾: 19½: 20: 20¾: 21¼] in

Length: (Long Version)
58 [60: 62: 64: 66: 68: 69: 71: 72] cm
22¾ [23½: 24½: 25¼: 26: 26¾: 27¼: 28: 28¼] in

40 [46: 52: 58: 61: 67: 70: 76: 82] cm
15¾ [18: 20½: 22¾: 24: 26½: 27½: 30: 32¼] in

ZOOM

○ ● ●

SIZE
To fit bust

71-76	81-86	91-97	102-107	112-117	122-127	132-137	142-147	152-157	cm
28-30	32-34	36-38	40-42	44-46	48-50	52-54	56-58	60-62	in

Actual bust measurement of garment

96	111	118	125	140	147	162	169	184	cm
38	43¾	46½	49½	55	58	63¾	66½	72¼	in

YARN
Big Wool

9	9	10	11	12	13	14	15	15	x 100gr

(photographed in Melon 094)

NEEDLES
1 pair 10mm (no 000) (US 15) needles

TENSION
11 sts and 15 rows to 10 cm measured over patt st using 10mm (US 15) needles.

EXTRAS
Stitch holder
Stitch markers

BACK
Using 10mm (US 15) needles, cast on 56 [62: 68: 72: 78: 84: 90: 94: 102] sts.
Next row (RS): *K1, P1, rep from * to end.
This row forms rib.
Work a further 4 times in rib, ending on a RS row and with WS facing for next row.
Next row (WS): Keeping rib correct throughout, dec [inc: dec: dec: inc: dec: inc: inc: inc] 1 st at end of row. 55 [63: 67: 71: 79: 83: 91: 95: 103] sts.
Next row (RS): K3, *wyif, sl 1 purlwise, wyib, K3, rep from * to end.
Next row (WS): K1, *wyif, sl 1 purlwise, wyib, K3, from * to last 2 sts, wyif, sl 1 purlwise, wyib, K1.
The last 2 rows form the cartridge belt rib patt.
Continue working in patt as set until work measures 42 [43: 43.5: 44: 44.5: 45: 45: 46: 46] cm from cast on, ending on a WS row and with RS facing for next row.
Next row (RS): Keeping patt correct throughout and incorporating new sts into the pattern, inc 1 st at each end. 57 [65: 69: 73: 81: 85: 93: 97: 105] sts.
Next row (WS): Patt to end.
Repeat these last 2 rows 3 times more. 63 [71: 75: 79: 87: 91: 99: 103: 111] sts.
Keeping patt correct throughout, continue without shaping until work measures 70 [72: 74: 76: 78: 80: 81: 83: 84] cm from cast on, ending on a WS row and with RS facing for next row.
Shoulder Shaping
Starting on a RS row and keeping patt correct throughout, cast off 6 [6: 7: 7: 8: 9: 10: 10: 11] sts at beg of next 2 rows. 51 [59: 61: 65: 71: 73: 79: 83: 89] sts.

Sizes 142-147 & 152-157 cm ONLY
Next row (RS): Cast off 10 [11] sts, patt until 19 [21] sts on RH needle, K2tog and turn, leaving rem sts on a stitch holder. 20 [22] sts.
Next row (WS): Dec 1 st at neck edge, patt to end. 19 [21] sts.
Next row: Cast off 10 [11] sts, patt to end. 9 [10] sts.
Next row: Patt to end.
Cast off rem sts.
With RS facing, rejoin yarn, cast off 21 sts for centre back neck, K2tog, patt to end. 30 [33] sts.
Next row (WS): Cast off 10 [11] sts, patt 18 [20] sts, K2tog. 19 [21] sts.
Next row: Patt to end.
Next row: Cast off 10 [11] sts, patt to end. 9 [10] sts.
Next row: Patt to end.
Cast off rem sts.

All other sizes
Starting on a RS row and keeping patt correct throughout, cast off 5 [6: 7: 7: 8: 8: 9] sts at beg of next 2 rows. 41 [47: 47: 51: 55: 57: 61] sts.
Next row (RS): Cast off 5 [6: 6: 7: 8: 8: 9] sts, patt until 4 [5: 5: 6: 7: 7: 8] sts on RH needle, K2tog and turn, leaving rem sts on a stitch holder. 5 [6: 6: 7: 8: 8: 9] sts.
Next row: Patt to end.
Cast off rem sts.
With RS facing, rejoin yarn, cast off 19 [21: 21: 21: 21: 23: 23] sts for centre back neck, K2tog, patt to end. 10 [12: 12: 14: 16: 16: 18] sts.
Next row (WS): Cast off 5 [6: 6: 7: 8: 8: 9] sts, patt to end. 5 [6: 6: 7: 8: 8: 9] sts.
Next row: Patt to end.
Cast off rem sts.

LEFT FRONT

Using 10mm (US 15) needles, cast on 18 [20: 22: 24: 28: 30: 32: 36: 38] sts.

Next row (RS): *K1, P1, rep from * to end.

This row forms rib.

Work a further 4 times in rib, ending on a RS row and with WS facing for next row.

Next row (WS): Keeping rib correct throughout, inc [inc: inc: inc: dec: dec: inc: dec: inc] 1 st at end of row. 19 [21: 23: 25: 27: 29: 33: 35: 39] sts.

With RS facing, place a stitch marker 0 [1: 0: 1: 0: 1: 1: 0: 0] st(s) in from both edges. These markers will set the edge sts worked in rev st st throughout.

Work in Cartridge Belt Rib patt as set for back until work measures 42 [43: 43.5: 44: 44.5: 45: 45: 46: 46] cm from cast on, ending on a WS row and with RS facing for next row.

Next row (RS): Keeping patt correct throughout and incorporating new sts into the pattern, inc 1 st at beg of next 4 RS rows. 23 [25: 27: 29: 31: 33: 37: 39: 43] sts. Keeping patt correct throughout, continue without shaping until work measures 70 [72: 74: 76: 78: 80: 81: 83: 84] cm from cast on, ending on a WS row and with RS facing for next row.

Shoulder Shaping

Next row (RS): Cast off 6 [6: 7: 7: 8: 9: 10: 10: 11] sts, patt to end. 17 [19: 20: 22: 23: 24: 27: 29: 32] sts.

Next row (WS): Patt to end.

Next row: Cast off 5 [6: 7: 7: 8: 8: 9: 10: 11] sts, patt to end. 12 [13: 13: 15: 15: 16: 18: 19: 21] sts.

Next row: Patt to end.

Next row: Cast off 5 [6: 6: 7: 8: 8: 9: 10: 11] sts, patt to end. 7 [7: 7: 8: 7: 8: 10: 10: 10] sts.

Next row: Patt to end.

Cast off rem sts.

RIGHT FRONT

Work as for left front until work measures 42 [43: 43.5: 44: 44.5: 45: 45: 46: 46] cm from beg, ending on a WS row and with RS facing for next row.

Next row (RS): Keeping patt correct throughout and incorporating new sts into the pattern, inc 1 st at end of next 4 RS rows. 23 [25: 27: 29: 31: 33: 37: 39: 43] sts. Keeping patt correct throughout, continue without shaping until work measures 70 [72: 74: 76: 78: 80: 81: 83: 84] cm from cast on, ending on a RS row and with WS facing for next row.

Shoulder Shaping

Next row (WS): Cast off 6 [6: 7: 7: 8: 9: 10: 10: 11] sts, patt to end. 17 [19: 20: 22: 23: 24: 27: 29: 32] sts.

Next row (RS): Patt to end.

Next row: Cast off 5 [6: 7: 7: 8: 8: 9: 10: 11] sts, patt to end. 12 [13: 13: 15: 15: 16: 18: 19: 21] sts.

Next row: Patt to end.

Next row: Cast off 5 [6: 6: 7: 8: 8: 9: 10: 11] sts, patt to end. 7 [7: 7: 8: 7: 8: 10: 10: 10] sts.

Next row: Patt to end.

Cast off rem sts.

SLEEVES

Join both shoulder seams using mattress stitch, and mark points along side seam edges 23 [24: 25.5: 27: 28.5: 30: 31: 32: 33] cm on either side of shoulder seams to denote base of armhole openings.

With RS facing and using 10mm (US15) needles, starting at underarm, pick up and knit 49 [51: 55: 59: 61: 65: 67: 69: 71] sts evenly along the armhole edge.

Place a stitch marker 1 [0: 0: 0: 1: 1: 0: 1: 0] st in from both edges. These markers will set the edge sts worked in rev st st throughout.

Starting with a WS row, work in Cartridge Rib patt as set for Back until sleeve measures 16 [16: 16: 16: 14: 14: 13: 13: 10] cm from armhole.

Cast off loosely.

MAKING UP

Press as described on the information page.
Join side and sleeve seams using mattress stitch.
Neckband
Using 10mm (US15) needle, cast on 13 sts.
Next row (RS): K2, * P1, K1, rep from * to last st, K1.
Next row (WS): K1, * P1, K1, rep from * to end.
These 2 rows form rib.
Work in rib until band, when slightly stretched, fits along right front opening edge, along back neck edge, then along left front opening edge, sewing into place as you go along.
Cast off in rib.

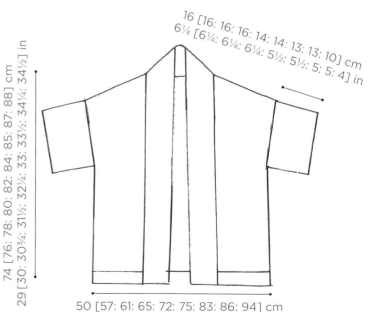

74 [76: 78: 80: 82: 84: 85: 87: 88] cm
29 [30: 30¾: 31½: 32¼: 33: 33½: 34¼: 34½] in

16 [16: 16: 16: 14: 14: 13: 13: 10] cm
6¼ [6¼: 6¼: 6¼: 5½: 5½: 5: 5: 4] in

50 [57: 61: 65: 72: 75: 83: 86: 94] cm
19¾ [22½: 24: 25½: 28¼: 29¾: 32½: 34: 36¾] in

SIZING GUIDE

SIZING

We have recently increased our size range to help you achieve the best fit for your knitwear. Our womenswear sizes now range from 28"/71cm through to 62"/157cm across the chest.

Dimensions in the charts below are body measurements, not garment dimensions. Therefore, please refer to the measuring guide to help you to determine which is the best size for you to knit.

To fit bust

28-30	32-34	36-38	40-42	44-46	48-50	52-54	56-58	60-62	inches
71-76	81-86	91-97	102-107	112-117	122-127	132-137	142-147	152-157	cm

To fit waist

20-22	24-26	28-30	32-34	36-38	40-42	44-46	48-50	52-54	inches
51-56	61-66	71-76	81-86	91-97	102-107	112-117	122-127	132-137	cm

To fit hips

30-31	34-36	38-40	42-44	46-48	50-52	54-56	58-60	62-64	inches
76-81	86-91	97-102	107-112	117-122	127-132	137-142	147-152	157-162	cm

SIZING & SIZE DIAGRAM NOTE

The instructions are given for the smallest size. Where they vary, work the figures in brackets for the larger sizes. One set of figures refers to all sizes.

Included with most patterns is a size diagram; see image below of the finished garment and its dimensions. The measurement shown at the bottom of each size diagram shows the garment width. The size diagram will also indicate how the garment is constructed. For example, if the garment has a drop shoulder, this will be reflected in the drawing.

To help you choose the size of garment to knit, please refer to the sizing guide. Generally, in the majority of designs, the welt width (at the cast-on edge of the garment) is the same width as the chest.

If you don't want to measure yourself, note the size of a similar shaped garment that you own and compare it with the size diagram given at the end of the pattern.

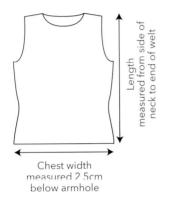

Length measured from side of neck to end of welt

Chest width measured 2.5cm below armhole

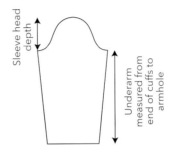

Sleeve head depth

Underarm measured from end of cuffs to armhole

MEASURING GUIDE

For maximum comfort and to ensure the correct fit when choosing a size to knit, please follow the tips below when checking your size. Measure yourself close to your body, over your underwear, and don't pull the tape measure too tight!

Bust/chest | measure around the fullest part of the bust/chest and across the shoulder blades.

Waist | measure around the natural waistline, just above the hip bones.

Hips | measure around the fullest part of the bottom.

Female model wears a dress size 10,
height 5'8
Garments knitted in 32 - 34"

Male model wears a chest size 46",
height 6'3
Garments knitted in 44 - 46"

Finally, once you have decided which size is best for you, please ensure that you achieve the tension required for the design you wish to knit.

Remember, if your tension is too loose, your garment will be bigger than the pattern size and you may use more yarn. If your tension is too tight, your garment could be smaller than the pattern size and you will have yarn left over.

Furthermore, if your tension is incorrect, the handle of your fabric will be too stiff or floppy and will not fit properly. It really does make sense to check your tension before starting every project.

TENSION

This is the size of your knitting. Most of the knitting patterns will have a tension quoted. This is how many stitches 10cm/4in in width and how many rows 10cm/4in in length to make a square. If your knitting doesn't match this, then your finished garment will not measure the correct size. To obtain the correct measurements for your garment, you must achieve the tension.

The tension quoted on a ball band is the manufacturer's average. For the manufacturer and designers to produce designs, they have to use a tension for you to be able to obtain the measurements quoted. It's fine not to be the average, but you need to know if you meet the average or not. Then you can make the necessary adjustments to obtain the correct measurements.

CHOOSING YARN

All the colours and textures, where do you start? Look for the thickness - how chunky do you want your finished garment? Sometimes it's colour that draws you to a yarn, or perhaps you have a pattern that requires a specific yarn. Check the washing/care instructions before you buy.

Yarn varies in thickness; there are various descriptions, such as DK and 4ply. These are examples of standard weights. There are a lot of yarns available that are not standard, so it helps to read the ball band to see what the recommended needle size is.

This will give you an idea of the approximate thickness. It is best to use the yarn recommended in the pattern.
Keep one ball band from each project so that you have a record of what you have used, and most importantly, how to care for your garment after it has been completed. Always remember to give the ball band with the garment if it is a gift.

The ball band normally provides you with the average tension and recommended needle sizes for the yarn, this may vary from what has been used in the pattern, always go with the pattern as the designer may change needles to obtain a certain look. The ball band also tells you the name of the yarn and what it is made of, the weight and approximate length of the ball of yarn, along with the shade and dye lot numbers. This is important as dye lots can vary, so you need to buy your yarn with matching dye lots.

PRESSING AND AFTERCARE

Having spent so long knitting your project, it can be a great shame not to look after it properly. Some yarns are suitable for pressing once you have finished to improve the look of the fabric. To find out this information, you will need to look on the yarn ball band, where there will be washing and care symbols.

Once you have checked to see if your yarn is suitable to be pressed and the knitting is a smooth texture (stocking stitch, for example), pin out and place a damp cloth onto the knitted pieces. Hold the steam iron (at the correct temperature) approximately 10cm/4in away from the fabric and steam. Keep the knitted pieces pinned in place until cool.

As a test, it is a good idea to wash your tension square in the way you would expect to wash your garment.

ABBREVIATIONS

alt	alternate
beg	begin(ning)
cm	centimetres
cont	continue
dec	decrease(s)(ing)
foll(s)	follow(s)(ing)
g	grams
g st	garter stitch (knit all rows)
in	inch(es)
inc	increase(s)(ing)
K	knit
Kfb	knit in front and back of stitch (makes 1stitch)
M1	make 1 stitch
meas	measures
mm	millimetres
P	purl
patt	pattern
psso	pass slipped stitch over
rem	remain(ing)
rep	repeat
RS	right side of work
Sl 1	slip 1 stitch
st st	stocking stitch (knit on RS rows, purl on WS rows)
st(s)	stitch(es)
tbl	through back of loop
tog	together
WS	wrong side of work